Leonardo DiCaprio

Other books in the People in the News series:

people
in the
NEWS

Leonardo DiCaprio

by Cherese Cartlidge

LUCENT BOOKS
A part of Gale, Cengage Learning

GALE
CENGAGE Learning

Detroit • New York • San Francisco • New Haven, Conn • Waterville, Maine • London

LIBRARY OF CONGRESS CATALOGING-IN-PUBLICATION DATA

Cartlidge, Cherese.
  Leonardo DiCaprio / by Cherese Cartlidge.
    p. cm. -- (People in the news)
  Includes bibliographical references and index.
  ISBN 978-1-4205-0427-9 (hardcover)
1. DiCaprio, Leonardo--Juvenile literature. 2. Motion picture actors and
actresses--United States--Juvenile literature. I. Title.
  PN2287.D4635C36 2011
  791.43'028'092--dc22
  [B]
                                                                    2010043806

Lucent Books
27500 Drake Rd
Farmington Hills MI 48331

ISBN-13: 978-1-4205-0427-9
ISBN-10: 1-4205-0427-4

Printed in the United States of America
1 2 3 4 5 6 7 15 14 13 12 11

Printed by Bang Printing, Brainerd, MN, 1st Ptg., 02/2011

Contents

Foreword

F ame and celebrity are alluring. People are drawn to those who walk in fame's spotlight, whether they are known for great accomplishments or for notorious deeds. The lives of the famous pique public interest and attract attention, perhaps because their experiences seem in some ways so different from, yet in other ways so similar to, our own.

Newspapers, magazines, and television regularly capitalize on this fascination with celebrity by running profiles of famous people. For example, television programs such as *Entertainment Tonight* devote all their programming to stories about entertainment and entertainers. Magazines such as *People* fill their pages with stories of the private lives of famous people. Even newspapers, newsmagazines, and television news frequently delve into the lives of well-known personalities. Despite the number of articles and programs, few provide more than a superficial glimpse at their subjects.

Lucent's People in the News series offers young readers a deeper look into the lives of today's newsmakers, the influences that have shaped them, and the impact they have had in their fields of endeavor and on other people's lives. The subjects of the series hail from many disciplines and walks of life. They include authors, musicians, athletes, political leaders, entertainers, entrepreneurs, and others who have made a mark on modern life and who, in many cases, will continue to do so for years to come.

These biographies are more than factual chronicles. Each book emphasizes the contributions, accomplishments, or deeds that have brought fame or notoriety to the individual and shows how that person has influenced modern life. Authors portray their subjects in a realistic, unsentimental light. For example, Bill Gates—the cofounder and chief executive officer of the software giant Microsoft—has been instrumental in making personal computers the most vital tool of the modern age. Few dispute his business savvy, his perseverance, or his technical expertise, yet critics say he is ruthless in his dealings with competitors and driven more by his desire to maintain Microsoft's dominance in the computer industry than by an interest in furthering technology.

In these books, young readers will encounter inspiring stories about real people who achieved success despite enormous obstacles. Oprah Winfrey—the most powerful, most watched, and wealthiest woman on television today—spent the first six years of her life in the care of her grandparents while her unwed mother sought work and a better life elsewhere. Her adolescence was colored by pregnancy at age fourteen, rape, and sexual abuse.

Each author documents and supports his or her work with an array of primary and secondary source quotations taken from diaries, letters, speeches, and interviews. All quotes are footnoted to show readers exactly how and where biographers derive their information and provide guidance for further research. The quotations enliven the text by giving readers eyewitness views of the life and accomplishments of each person covered in the People in the News series.

In addition, each book in the series includes photographs, annotated bibliographies, timelines, and comprehensive indexes. For both the casual reader and the student researcher, the People in the News series offers insight into the lives of today's newsmakers—people who shape the way we live, work, and play in the modern age.

The Kid from the Wrong Side of the Tracks

Leonardo DiCaprio is among the most sought-after actors of his generation. He is one of the biggest box-office attractions in the world and earns at least $20 million per picture. Some people may find it difficult to believe that the thirty-something brooding superstar once sold toy cars in TV commercials at age fourteen. From there, he went on to become a teen idol, first on the TV sitcom *Growing Pains* and later in a series of critically acclaimed movies. In fact, media magazine *Extra!* recently ranked him as number twenty-five on its list of the top fifty greatest teen stars of all time.

By the time he was nineteen years old, DiCaprio had been nominated for both an Academy Award and a Golden Globe Award for Best Supporting Actor, a degree of recognition that few actors achieve in a lifetime of work. But this was only the beginning. The worldwide hysteria that erupted over DiCaprio after his 1997 performance in the blockbuster *Titanic* has been compared to Beatlemania, the unprecedented frenzy over the British rock band the Beatles in the 1960s. DiCaprio is more than a cult phenomenon or a flash-in-the-pan superstar. He has proved himself to be a dedicated and talented actor who has lived up to the potential he showed from a young age.

DiCaprio seems to have been born to be an actor. The talent and ability he displays seem to come to him naturally. As the casting

Fans clamor for an autograph from Leonardo DiCaprio, who has grown from humble roots to become an international movie star.

director of *Romeo + Juliet* (1996) explains: "He has an innate ability to get under the skin of a character. He's one of the most instinctual young actors around today."[1] DiCaprio's instinct as an actor has allowed him to bring a wide variety of characters to life on-screen. Diane Keaton, who costarred with DiCaprio in *Marvin's Room* in 1996, once called him a chameleon for his ability to take on such a range of complex roles so convincingly.

From Rags to Riches

It is fortunate that DiCaprio was born with natural acting skill, because his meager Los Angeles upbringing did not provide him with many opportunities. In fact, his is a true rags-to-riches story. He grew up with his mother in a seedy neighborhood in East Hollywood. It was a rough place, and he was exposed to violence, drugs, theft, and prostitution from the time he was very young.

He has described his neighborhood as a "hellhole," saying, "It was really crazy. My mom and I lived in one of the seediest places on Earth." Young Leo was frequently exposed to disturbing scenes of drug use and public sex: "I remember, at five years old, having this guy with a trench coat, needles and crack, corner me. I'd see pushers peddling drugs, and prostitutes on drugs. It was pretty terrifying. There were rough kids. I got beat up a lot."[2]

After his parents separated, his mother had to work at a variety of odd jobs to support herself and her son. It seemed there was never enough money, and DiCaprio learned early that money was the key to rising above their meager existence. In fact, it was the desire to provide a better life for his mother that motivated DiCaprio to go into acting in the first place. Living near Hollywood, even in the bad neighborhood where he grew up, it was inevitable that he would discover the glitz and glamour of an actor's lifestyle. Once he learned how much money successful actors earned, he decided acting was the best way to escape the poverty and desperation of his neighborhood. Although breaking into show business was harder than he expected, he never gave up on his dream of becoming an actor and helping his mother find a better life.

Lucky Leo

DiCaprio has never forgotten his own humble beginnings, both off and on the screen. His rough childhood has motivated him to help disadvantaged children in both the United States and abroad. He has used his fame and wealth as an environmental activist, to protect endangered species, and to improve struggling peoples' standard of living. Despite all he has accomplished, he still thinks of himself as the kid from the wrong side of the tracks who lucked out.

Alan Thicke, who costarred with DiCaprio on *Growing Pains*, says he and the rest of the cast always knew DiCaprio would hit it big one day. "We had the sense then that nothing was ever going to stop him," Thicke later recalled. "He just lit up the place."[3] Today DiCaprio continues to light up whatever project he commits himself to. That light is poised to keep on shining for a very long time.

Chapter 1

A Born Actor

Leonardo Wilhelm DiCaprio was born in Los Angeles on November 11, 1974. He is the only child of George and Irmelin Idenbirken DiCaprio. His name is a reflection of his heritage—his father is Italian American, and his mother is a German immigrant. Irmelin chose his middle name, Wilhelm, because that was her father's first name. The inspiration for her son's first name came to Irmelin in a more unusual way. One day while she was pregnant, Irmelin visited the Uffizi Gallery, a museum in Florence, Italy. As she admired a painting by Leonardo da Vinci, she felt a strong kick from her unborn son. She took this as a sign and decided to name her son after the famous artist.

George and Irmelin met as students at the City College of New York. They were part of the counterculture movement of the 1960s. George worked as an underground cartoonist, producing and distributing comic books and alternative literature in the Los Angeles area. Irmelin worked as a legal secretary. The DiCaprios had very little money, and having a child put an additional strain on their relationship. Less than a year after Leo's birth, George and Irmelin decided to separate. Although their marriage had not lasted, they remained close and cooperated in raising their son.

"The Ghettos of Hollywood"

After his parents split up, Leo lived with his mother in a derelict part of Echo Park, a neighborhood between downtown Los Angeles and Hollywood. The low-rent neighborhood attracted struggling artists, writers, and musicians. It was also plagued by drugs and gangs. "I lived in the ghettos of Hollywood," DiCaprio said years later. "It was a disgusting place to be."[4] As a boy, Leo saw drug deals, drug addicts, prostitutes, and a lot of violence.

DiCaprio embraces his mother, Irmelin, at a movie promotion event in 1995. He has spoken of his close relationship with his parents as a highlight of his childhood.

Leo's Oma

Leonardo DiCaprio has a good relationship with both his parents, and he was also especially close to his maternal grandmother when he was growing up. His grandparents had lived in the United States for thirty years but moved back to Germany when DiCaprio was a child. He visited them each summer in Germany, still his favorite vacation spot, and fondly remembers the potato pancakes his grandmother used to make for him. He called her "Oma," which is German for "grandmother." In fact, it was she who taught him German, which he speaks fluently. He took her, along with his mother, to the London opening of *Titanic* in 1997. After he became world-famous, he still maintained a close relationship with his Oma, visiting her whenever his schedule allowed. She also visited the set whenever he was in Europe working on a movie. And she and his mother had a brief cameo together in one scene in *Blood Diamond* (2006)—DiCaprio walks past them as they stand talking together outside an airport. DiCaprio was deeply saddened in 2008 by the death of his Oma, who was ninety-three.

DiCaprio had an especially close relationship with his "Oma," Helene Indenbirken, left, who is shown at a movie premier with his mother, Irmelin, in 2002.

He recalls being cornered by a crack dealer when he was five years old and frequently getting beaten up by other kids. "It was pretty terrifying,"[5] he told an interviewer in 2009.

In spite of his parents' divorce and the rough neighborhood he lived in, Leo enjoyed a very close relationship with both his parents, who offered him plenty of love and support. Leo once told an interviewer, "My parents are so a part of my life, they're like my legs."[6] George frequently took Leo to movies and museums, and Leo spent time at his father's new house. Leo considers his father to be one of the most interesting people he knows. He describes him as a bohemian and "a diehard left-wing hippie with long freak hair and a beard."[7] He recalls attending parades with his father, both of them dressed up as "mudmen," smeared with mud and carrying sticks. George was so involved in his son's life that Leo never felt like he was missing out on a relationship with his father. In addition, after his father moved in with another woman, Leo gained a stepbrother, Adam Farrar, with whom he became close friends.

Leo also has a great deal of respect for his mother, whom he calls "a walking miracle"[8] for her determination to survive. Irmelin was born in Germany during World War II, in an air raid shelter during a bombing raid in 1943, and was separated from her parents for several weeks as a toddler at the end of the war. She immigrated to the United States with her family as a child during the 1950s. Her parents lived in the United States until 1985, when they returned to Germany. Although there was never much money when Leo was growing up, his mother managed to take him to Germany frequently to visit his grandparents, with whom he had an especially close relationship.

"He Was Kind of a Dork"

Leo's mother tried to shelter him from their dangerous environment by enrolling him in a school that was in a better neighborhood. She therefore drove him to school in Westwood, a more upscale part of Los Angeles. It was an hour's drive each way—which meant four hours of driving a day for Irmelin. She did not mind sacrificing this time or scrimping and saving from her paycheck for her son, because not only was the Corinne A. Seeds University Elementary School in a better neighborhood, it catered

DiCaprio, shown here at about age fourteen, attended a school for gifted and creative children, but he was not a good student.

to gifted and creative children. Leo took summer classes there in performing arts, and he later attended a highly ranked magnet school, the Los Angeles Center for Enriched Studies.

Overall, Leo was not a good student. He had trouble sitting still and doing his work. He liked history and drama and did well in those classes, but not in others, especially math. He admits that he sometimes cheated in order to pass math. In addition, he acted out in school. He often made jokes and wisecracks during class and put on performances to get the attention of the teachers and the other students. He had a talent for mimicry and entertained his classmates with, for example, Michael Jackson impressions and moonwalks. Another impression, however, nearly got him into a lot of trouble—he drew a swastika on his forehead one day to imitate mass murderer Charles Manson. His father had to go to the school and explain that Leo had meant no harm and did not really understand the seriousness of what he had done.

Leo's constant need for attention interfered with his ability to learn. The clowning around also made it hard for other kids to accept him. Because he was small for his age and was from a bad neighborhood, Leo never felt like he fit in with the other kids. He was often teased. One female classmate from high school recalls, "He was kind of a dork, like a little wimpy guy."[9] Leo attended John Marshall High School in the Los Feliz area of Los Angeles until his junior year, when he left school altogether.

A Family Affair

Leo did not have a lot of friends growing up and instead spent most of his time with his parents. They frequently took him for pony rides and to museums and concerts. Among his favorite memories from childhood are the three birthday parties his parents gave him at a train museum in California. There, Leo and the few friends he did have would play on the abandoned train cars.

Leo also loved to watch movies. As a young child, he developed an affinity for actors Robert De Niro, Al Pacino, and Jack Nicholson. He counts *Taxi Driver* (starring De Niro in an Oscar-nominated role) as one of his favorite movies of all time. Aside from watching movies, he liked to play pool, inline skate, and shoot hoops. He also liked to play video games. His favorite foods included pasta and lemonade. His taste in music and reading material seem to gravitate toward the old-fashioned. His favorite books as a child and teen were *Huckleberry Finn* by Mark Twain and *The Old Man and the Sea* by Ernest Hemingway. His favorite bands included Led Zeppelin, Pink Floyd, and the Beatles.

Leo's parents raised him to love animals, and he had a Rottweiler named Rocky. He was especially interested in anything to do with nature and evolution and for a while he wanted to be a marine biologist. He also loved to travel, especially to Germany to visit his mother's parents. "When I was young, I used to have this thing where I wanted to see everything," he says. "I used to think, 'How can I die without seeing every inch of this world?'"[10] For a while he thought he might like to be a travel agent, but "what I really wanted was to travel and see all the different animals that were on the verge of extinction."[11]

A Hard Lesson

Leonardo DiCaprio grew up in a rough neighborhood where he learned several hard lessons. One lesson came when he was eight years old and went outside with a pair of two-dollar bills, which he thought were cool because they were uncommon. He was so proud of the bills that he opened his wallet and showed them to another boy he saw in the alley. The boy then tricked him by saying there was a whole pile of money under a dumpster and telling him to bend down to look for it. DiCaprio explains that as soon as he had his head on the ground, the other boy, who was bigger than he was, kicked him, grabbed his wallet, and ran off. DiCaprio, his nose bloodied, chased the other boy for three blocks, to no avail. He says, "I never [got] my two-dollar bills back. But I came to understand money at an early age."

Quoted in Cal Fussman, "How Do You Become Leo DiCaprio?" *Esquire*, February 26, 2010. www.esquire.com/features/leonardo-dicaprio-quotes-0310?click=main_sr#ixzz0v6Saxphz.

The Acting Bug

Marine biology, travel, and endangered animals were not the only career paths young Leo had in mind. His parents had always encouraged and supported his creative side, and he thought from an early age that he would like to be an actor. He says, however, that as a child he did not think this was a realistic goal: "I never realised acting was a possibility. I thought it was a secret club only the privileged few were part of. I thought that maybe I could get a commercial here or there, but to have a career as an actor? Forget it."[12]

In fact, Leo's first experience in show business did not turn out well. When he was five years old, he was scheduled to be one of the

DiCaprio auditions for casting agents in 1991. His first acting jobs were in commercials, where he usually played roles written for boys much younger than he was.

children in the frequently changing cast of *Romper Room*, a popular children's TV series that ran from 1953 to 1994. His behavior on the set was so disruptive that he was fired the very first day. Leo recalls how hyper and difficult to control he was: "I ran up to the camera and started shaking it, saying, 'Look at me!'"[13]

Performing came naturally to Leo. His grandmother recalls that when he was a child, the family could not watch TV because he would always be in front of the screen, clowning around to get attention. In fact, she told him once that he had been an actor from the time he was born. It seemed only a matter of time before something would inspire Leo to get in front of a camera again.

His inspiration came when Leo was fourteen years old and his stepbrother, Adam, did a commercial for Golden Grahams breakfast cereal. Adam was paid fifty thousand dollars for the commercial. Leo decided he wanted to earn money in the same way. He says his main reason for wanting to earn a lot of money was his mother—he felt she deserved to live in a better place than the neighborhood where he grew up.

The first step was to get an agent. Leo's parents arranged interviews with talent agents but had some difficulty finding one that would sign him. One agent suggested that Leo change his name to Lenny Williams because it was less ethnic sounding, but Leo refused. Eventually, a family friend helped Leo get signed with an agency, and he started to audition. It was rough going at first. He experienced the typical rejection that most unknown, aspiring actors experience. At one audition, for example, he was turned away because he had the wrong haircut. He auditioned for fifty commercials before he finally landed one. He was fourteen, but he played a ten-year-old in his first commercial, for Matchbox toy cars. Looking younger than his age proved to be an advantage for Leo. He had better memorization skills, was more mature, and was better able to follow directions than the younger children he was competing against for parts.

Leo appeared in thirty commercials by the time he was six-teen, including fifteen for Matchbox cars, and others for bubble gum, toys, and cereal. The money he earned allowed him and his

"A Great Actor"

As a child, Leo loved to go to the movies with his dad, which he did often. When he was thirteen, his father took him to see *Midnight Run*, which starred one of his favorite actors, Robert De Niro.

> I remember the first time I saw Robert De Niro up on the screen. I was thirteen years old.... My father and I went to see *Midnight Run*, and I remember my dad in the beginning of the film pointing to the screen and saying, "You see that guy there? Now that guy is cool. His name is Robert De Niro. You wanna watch a great actor, you remember his face."

Quoted in American Film Institute, "Leonardo DiCaprio Salutes Robert De Niro." www.afi.com/video/VideoPlayer.aspx?videoid=MUV2UeqQYEI.

mother to move to a nicer neighborhood in Los Angeles. Now that he had helped his mother move to a nicer place, Leo had another goal: expanding beyond commercials and landing parts on television shows.

Guest Starring Leonardo DiCaprio

Leo's television series debut came in 1990 with his appearance in a two-part episode of *The New Lassie*, in which he played a kid trying to win a bike race. Other guest appearances followed on episodes of *The Outsiders* and *Roseanne*. He also made short educational films such as *How to Deal with a Parent Who Takes Drugs* and *Mickey's Safety Club*. Although he was pleased with the money he was making, he wanted a larger role, something that would last longer than a single appearance. He got that chance in 1990

DiCaprio, far right, poses with the cast of Parenthood, *a 1990 television series on NBC that gained him notice as a heartthrob among teen girls.*

when he was cast as a recurring character on the NBC soap opera *Santa Barbara.* Leo played Mason Capwell, a teenage alcoholic. He found acting in a soap challenging because each hour-long episode was filmed live every day. He had to memorize new lines each night. Although he learned a lot from the experience, when it ended he said that he would never do another soap opera.

Appearing regularly on TV programs was a big boost to his acting career. It offered him another benefit: It enabled him to finish his high school education. He had dropped out of high school, but by law, child actors must spend half the day either in school or with a tutor. Although he had never been a good student, Leo's intellectual side thrived with the one-on-one attention he received from his tutor. For the first time in his life he excelled at academics.

He also began to receive accolades for his acting. For his work on *Santa Barbara*, Leo was nominated for the Young Artist Award for Best Young Actor in a Daytime Series. His role on the show lasted only a few months, but he soon got another break when he was cast as a regular in *Parenthood* alongside David Arquette and Ed Begley Jr. This 1990 NBC sitcom was based on the hit 1989 feature film of the same name. Leo made a good impression on audiences, particularly teen girls. His face began to be featured on the covers of teen magazines like *Bop* and *16*. He received another nomination for his work on *Parenthood*, the Young Artist Award for Best Young Actor Starring in a Television Series. Although Leo was well received, the show itself did not do well in the ratings. When *Parenthood* was cancelled after only four months, he quickly began to look for another series. He did not have to look for long.

Growing Pains

In 1991, shortly after *Parenthood* was cancelled, Leo was cast as a regular on the ABC sitcom *Growing Pains*. He joined the series, one of the biggest hits of the 1980s, in its seventh and final season. Revolving around the fictional Seaver family, *Growing Pains* starred Alan Thicke and Joanna Kerns as the parents of three children, played by Kirk Cameron, Tracy Gold, and Jeremy Miller. The boyishly handsome Cameron had gained teen idol status during the show's run. But Cameron was entering his twenties; the show's producers decided to introduce a new character who was a little younger in hopes of reviving the interest of young female fans. They cast Leo as a homeless boy named Luke Bower who comes to live with the Seavers. Although Leo gained a lot of attention in this role and was nominated for the Young Artist Award for Best Young Actor Co-starring in a Television Series, *Growing Pains* slipped in the ratings and was cancelled in 1992.

By then, Leo had started auditioning for roles in feature films. He appeared in *Critters 3* (1991), a flop that went straight to video. In *Poison Ivy 2* (1992), he appeared briefly in the opening scene playing a character listed merely as "Guy" in the credits. Although his first two movie roles turned out to

DiCaprio's popularity grew after his stint on the television series Growing Pains, and his public appearances included the 1992 MTV Rock N' Jock basketball game to benefit the Pediatric AIDS Foundation.

be mostly forgettable, it was only the beginning for him. He could not have known it at the time, but his career was about to experience the big breakthrough he had been dreaming of.

Chapter 2

Playing the Troubled Teen

By the time he was eighteen years old, DiCaprio had begun to appear in larger movie roles, bringing with him the troubled teen persona he had developed in TV roles. At first he played supporting parts, but directors and producers quickly cast him in leading roles. From the start, his performances as troubled characters won critical acclaim, and one of his earliest roles earned him the highest praise for an actor of any age—an Academy Award nomination.

The Audition That Changed Everything

DiCaprio's breakout movie role was in *This Boy's Life* (1993). Set in the Pacific Northwest in the 1950s, the movie is based on American author Tobias Wolff's autobiography. It depicts his struggles growing up with an emotionally and physically abusive stepfather. DiCaprio starred alongside Ellen Barkin, who played his mother, and Robert De Niro, who played his stepfather.

DiCaprio was only sixteen years old when he auditioned for the role of Toby Wolff. The process was long and difficult, lasting four months and involving a series of intense interviews and seven separate auditions. He was one of the first actors to read for the part. Although the director, Michael Caton-Jones, was immediately impressed by the young DiCaprio, Caton-Jones

Less Is More

At the televised *31st American Film Institute Life Achievement Award Tribute to Robert De Niro* in 2003, Leonardo DiCaprio recalled his audition for *This Boy's Life*—as well as a lesson he learned from the great actor:

> Before this critical audition, I watched as many of his films as I could, and I asked myself over and over and over again, "What is the one quality that he would see in me that he would respect?" And then it came to me. Menace. I knew that I needed to walk into that audition and be a menacing force to be reckoned with. We were midpoint in the scene where De Niro's character is actually ramming a mustard jar into my eye and asking me repeatedly, "Is it empty? Is it empty?" I knew this was my moment. I got up from the couch, walked across the room, looked him dead in the eye, pointed in his face, and shouted at the top of my lungs, "NOOOO!"
>
> Silence.... This De Niro guy was stunned. And then it dawned on me, he wasn't stone faced because of my awe-inspiring performance, he was trying to contain his laughter.... He turned to me and said, "That was good, that was good. Uh ... on that last line, why don't you just try to ... just take it down a notch. One notch." ... So I did. I took it down a notch. And I learned a valuable lesson, that some things are good only to a certain degree.

Quoted in American Film Institute, "Leonardo DiCaprio Salutes Robert De Niro." www.afi.com/video/VideoPlayer.aspx?videoid=MUV2UeqQYEI.

was reluctant to make a decision so early in the casting process. "I knew he was it, but when someone reads for you that early, you don't believe it," he said. "So we tried loads and loads of young actors, but we came right back to Leonardo."[14] In fact, DiCaprio beat out over four hundred other young actors for the part in what *Rolling Stone* editor Brian Hiatt referred to as "the movie that changed the course of his career."[15]

Costarring in a movie with Robert De Niro was a huge opportunity for DiCaprio. De Niro was not only one of his favorite actors, but a well-respected two-time Academy Award winner. DiCaprio recalls the impact of working with De Niro in *This Boy's Life*: "It was a complete learning experience for me, watching De Niro acting every day. Like a drama school. That showed me what real acting is all about and it molded me for the rest of my career."[16]

Working on his first major film was not easy for DiCaprio. There were times when his inexperience and youthfulness were obvious to others, including the director. "I didn't know how to conduct myself on a film set,"[17] DiCaprio remembers. The role itself was difficult, as well. Playing the part of Toby was challenging mentally, emotionally, and physically, because De Niro's character, Dwight, was verbally as well as physically abusive. In one pivotal scene, in which Dwight physically assaults Toby, De Niro and DiCaprio had to throw each other around the set. DiCaprio recalls getting his fair share of bruises during the filming of the movie.

The movie was not a big box office hit, grossing only about $5 million when it was released in the United States in 1993. Critics, however, praised the film and especially DiCaprio's performance. The *New York Daily News* called it "the breakthrough performance of the decade."[18] In fact, many reviewers implied that DiCaprio had outperformed De Niro in the film. *People* magazine also complimented the young actor, saying that "Leonardo DiCaprio, in his first major movie role, carried the film with impressive ease."[19] Film critic Roger Ebert added: "The movie is successful largely because [DiCaprio] is a good enough actor to hold his own in his scenes with De Niro."[20] For his performance, DiCaprio earned the New Generation Award from the Los Angeles Film Critics Association.

What's Eating Gilbert Grape

Thanks largely to the recognition DiCaprio earned for *This Boy's Life*, offers for movie roles multiplied. He considered a part in the comedy-fantasy *Hocus Pocus* (1993), starring Bette Midler

DiCaprio joins co-star Johnny Depp, right, at a screening of What's Eating Gilbert Grape? *in 1993. DiCaprio's performance earned him Academy Award and Golden Globe nominations.*

and Sarah Jessica Parker. It was a role he was wise to turn down; *Hocus Pocus* bombed at the box office. Instead, DiCaprio accepted a supporting role in *What's Eating Gilbert Grape?* (1993). He was to play the part of Arnie Grape, an eighteen-year-old boy who is intellectually impared. Cast in the role of Arnie's big brother, Gilbert, was Johnny Depp. The popular Depp, known for quirky roles in *Edward Scissorhands* and *Benny & Joon*, was a hot property in Hollywood after his own recent jump from television to movies.

DiCaprio's physical features almost kept him from being cast in the film: he was considered too handsome to play the mentally disabled Arnie. Said director Lasse Hallström, "I needed someone who wasn't good looking. But of all the actors who auditioned for the role of Arnie, Leonardo was the most observant."[21] During filming, DiCaprio wore a mouth appliance to help alter the shape of his face. He went further than just changing his appearance to prepare for the role, however. DiCaprio visited homes for the intellectually disabled to observe and learn how to move and react naturally. "I had to really research and get into the mind of somebody with a disability like that," he says. "So I spent a few days at a home for mentally retarded teens. We just talked and I watched their mannerisms. People have these expectations that mentally retarded children are really crazy, but it's not so. It's refreshing to see them because everything's so new to them."[22]

DiCaprio's own hyperactive, attention-seeking nature, which had once gotten him thrown off the set of *Romper Room*, now came in handy for this movie. Arnie's character had very few lines in the script, so DiCaprio improvised much of his performance. He praised the director and his costars for allowing him the freedom "to run amok in all these scenes."[23] It was this freedom to do whatever struck him at the spur of the moment that helped DiCaprio make Arnie Grape such a memorable character.

The movie earned mixed but generally positive reviews. DiCaprio's sensational performance, however, was highly praised. Once again, critics suggested that DiCaprio had stolen the film from a better-known and more experienced costar. Movie reviewer David Ansen praised Depp's performance, calling it "subtly winning," then added, "but the performance that will take your breath away is DiCaprio's. A lot of actors have taken flashy stabs at playing retarded characters and no one, old or young, has ever done it better. He's exasperatingly, heartbreakingly real."[24]

"He's So Good, It's Scary"

The critics were not the only ones to praise DiCaprio for his portrayal of Arnie Grape. His performance in *What's Eating Gilbert Grape?* earned him Academy Award and Golden Globe nominations for Best Supporting Actor. At nineteen years old, he was one of the youngest actors ever to be nominated for an Academy Award. It was an incredible honor for such a young, relatively inexperienced actor. Although he did not win either prestigious award, he did receive two others for this performance—the Chicago Film Critics Association and the National Board of Review awards for Best Supporting Actor.

Suddenly, DiCaprio was viewed as a genuine film star, and the movie offers began pouring in. He considered all offers carefully and rejected those that seemed too commercial, preferring instead to play characters that were unique in some way. Because he was so selective, he almost turned down the role of the Kid in *The Quick and the Dead* (1995) because he could not imagine himself appearing in a Western. Sharon Stone, however, who coproduced as well as starred in the film, was determined to cast him, saying, "'He's so good, it's scary."[25] She was so adamant about having him

DiCaprio appears with author Jim Carroll, left, who was portrayed by DiCaprio in The Basketball Diaries in 1995.

in the movie that she even gave up part of her salary to pay his. Stone's persistence paid off, and she won over DiCaprio, who agreed to appear in the film. The character he plays is deeply troubled because his own father will not acknowledge him as his son, and the Kid goes to tragic lengths to win his father's recognition and approval. The all-star cast members, including Gene Hackman and Russell Crowe as well as Stone, were praised for their performances, and DiCaprio also received positive notices for his work. The movie itself, however, bombed at the box office and was widely panned by the critics.

DiCaprio received considerably more praise for his next film, *The Basketball Diaries* (1995). Like *This Boy's Life*, this movie was based on an autobiography. It portrays the early life of musician and poet Jim Carroll and his descent from basketball star into heroin use and prostitution. In *The Basketball Diaries* DiCaprio found himself once again playing a troubled teen facing serious conflicts. Yet the movie marked a couple of firsts for him. It was his first leading, rather than supporting, role. It was also the first film in which he was involved with the casting and other decision making.

The movie itself had only a mediocre turn at the box office, earning a modest $2.5 million. Although it received poor reviews—most critics said it was disappointing and poorly directed—DiCaprio was praised for his performance. Edward Guthmann of the *San Francisco Chronicle* wrote, "He seems incapable of making a false move on screen."[26]

Weathering Criticism

His next film, however, was not well received by either the critics or the public. In *Total Eclipse* (1995), DiCaprio plays the nineteenth-century poet Arthur Rimbaud. It was a daring role, because the film depicts Rimbaud abusing alcohol and drugs and entering into a homosexual relationship with another poet, the older Paul Verlaine. Most critics complained that he played the role of the troubled and impulsive young Rimbaud too closely to his role in *The Basketball Diaries*. Another criticism of the film was that DiCaprio delivered his lines with his own Southern California accent, and not with a French accent. A review in *Screen International* went even further, calling DiCaprio's portrayal of Rimbaud "a potentially career-damaging performance."[27]

Appearing in two films in a row that did so poorly at the box office might have discouraged another actor. DiCaprio, however, was not bothered. He explains: "I'm really glad I did those two movies. I'm proud of my work in them. In five years nobody will remember any of the bad reviews, and my work in them will be seen as part of all my work. I'm not worried about that."[28]

It seems he was right not to worry. He bounced back from the criticism in his next film, the drama *Marvin's Room* (1996), in which he costarred with Diane Keaton, Meryl Streep, and Robert De Niro. In fact, it was the chance to work with De Niro again that

Choosing Scripts

Leonardo DiCaprio is very particular about the roles he takes. He prefers small, artistic films with an edge rather than films that are designed to be commercially successful. From the beginning of his career, he has relied on his father's advice when choosing which scripts to pursue. For example, it was his father who advised him to reject a role in the 1993 flop *Hocus Pocus* (1993) and instead audition for the more challenging (and successful) *What's Eating Gilbert Grape?*

DiCaprio says he and his father almost always have the same opinion about scripts: "He recommends the [scripts] he thinks I should take a look at. He's the person I most look up to in this world, he's the most intelligent guy I've ever met, so naturally I respect his opinion more than anybody's." Among the other scripts George DiCaprio has recommended his son pursue are *This Boy's Life, Total Eclipse*, and *Romeo + Juliet*.

Quoted in Brian J. Robb, *The Leonardo DiCaprio Album*. London: Plexus, 1998, p. 69.

DiCaprio starred opposite Claire Danes, left, as the title characters in Romeo + Juliet, *in a modern film adaption of Shakespeare's play released in 1996.*

convinced DiCaprio to do the film, although they only appear in one scene together. He plays Hank, Meryl Streep's teenage son who has recently been released from a mental institution after having set the family's home on fire. The rebellious Hank has trouble relating to adults, especially his mother, but finds a warm and satisfying relationship with his aunt, played by Diane Keaton. *Marvin's Room* brought DiCaprio further critical acclaim. He and the rest of the cast were nominated for a Screen Actors Guild Award for Best Ensemble Cast, and DiCaprio won a Chlotrudis Award for Best Supporting Actor.

DiCaprio hit it big with his next film as well, playing the tragic male lead in *Romeo + Juliet* (1996). Even this classic role was a bit of typecasting for DiCaprio; Romeo is yet another impulsive, conflicted teenager in a complicated and difficult situation. At first DiCaprio was leery of taking on a Shakespearean role, but his father persuaded him to look at the script. Part of what attracted DiCaprio to the film is that this hip, modern adaptation is drastically different from Shakespeare's original. The dialogue has been cut, guns and gangs replace swords and feuding families, and the setting has been moved from the Italian city of Verona to the fictional Los Angeles–like city of Verona Beach. Although film critic Roger Ebert called the production a "very bad idea,"[29] *Romeo + Juliet* was very successful at the box office, bringing in close to $150 million worldwide. The movie also brought DiCaprio international attention, made him a sex symbol, and put him on the A-list of Hollywood actors.

Growing Up

DiCaprio had successfully made the transition to leading man, and now, thanks to *Romeo + Juliet*, was seen as a romantic lead. Romance and maturity was reflected in his personal life, too. Although he continued living with his mother in Los Feliz for several years after his career took off, by 1997 he had moved into his own home in Los Angeles. He had also begun dating. His name was linked to a succession of actresses and models, including Juliette Lewis, Sara Gilbert, Bijou Phillips, Alicia Silverstone, Bridget Hall and Claire Danes. While each of these relationships were covered with great interest by the celebrity press, DiCaprio claimed they were all merely friendships. In 1995 he began his first long-term relationship, with model Kristen Zang, about whom he said, "I can't wait to see her at the end of the day. She's the cutest girl in the world."[30]

Despite growing up in real life, he continued to play roles that were younger than his actual age, thanks to his youthful appearance. Due in large part to being nominated for the Academy Award so young, and to the attention he was getting for his role in *Romeo + Juliet*, he was now in a position to choose from a variety of very desirable roles. In fact, he appeared in seven

Although he had been romantically linked with several young actresses, DiCaprio's first long-term girlfriend was model Kristen Zang, right, whom he began dating in 1995.

films released between 1993 and 1996. Yet even as successful as Leonardo DiCaprio already was, no one could have predicted the explosion that his next film was about to ignite.

Chapter 3

Leo-Mania

Romeo + *Juliet* helped the public see DiCaprio as a romantic leading man, but his next movie—the record-setting blockbuster *Titanic* (1997)—would cement his reputation as the ultimate chivalrous hero. During this period of his life, he was at the height of his popularity, sometimes referred to as "Leo-mania." DiCaprio's performance in the highest-grossing film in history earned him a place among the top actors of his generation and sparked an explosion of international fame. Yet the role of Jack Dawson was one that he almost did not take.

Finding Jack Dawson

DiCaprio has always been reluctant to appear in mainstream, commercial movies, and *Titanic* was no exception. From his earliest days as an actor, when the scripts and movie offers came pouring in after his successes in *This Boy's Life* and *What's Eating Gilbert Grape?*, he has always been very careful about the roles he accepts. He explains how particular he was about sifting through thousands of offers to decide which ones to take: "There are a lot of people who have gotten good roles at a young age and their careers later slopped out. Meaning no disrespect to anybody, I wanted to hold out for what I believed were good projects, I set some standards and hoped."[31]

British actress Kate Winslet was instrumental in convincing DiCaprio that he had to take the part. She had already been cast as the female lead, playing the part of Rose DeWitt Bukater. She desperately wanted to play opposite Leonardo DiCaprio.

DiCaprio performs as Jack Dawson opposite Kate Winslet's Rose, left, in Titanic. Winslet helped convince DiCaprio to take the role.

In fact, she said she would not do the film without him. "I was thinking," she explains, "'I'm going to persuade him to do this, because I'm not going to do it without him, and that's all there is to it.' Because he's brilliant. He's a genius."[32] Winslet was in luck; she and DiCaprio both happened to attend the 1996 Cannes Film Festival in France. She tracked him down at his hotel and made her case to him in person.

Winslet was so persistent about DiCaprio taking the role of Jack Dawson that he finally relented. It was more than her determination, however, that appealed to him:

> I didn't want to be prejudiced against this movie just because it was big. What appealed to me when I met [director] Jim [Cameron] is he knew that although this is a kind of an epic piece, it is glued together by the Jack and Rose characters. That's what people are really going to be attached to, no matter how good the special effects are. The ship sinking wasn't going to be anything without this love story.[33]

The "Real" Jack Dawson?

One historical fact that did not escape *Titanic's* young fans is that there was a real J. Dawson who sailed on the RMS *Titanic*. He was a twenty-four-year-old from Dublin, Ireland, who worked in the ship's boiler room. Like the majority of men aboard the doomed ship, the real Dawson died the night the *Titanic* sank. The real Dawson's first name was Joseph, however, and the character of Jack was not based on him at all—the similarity in the names is merely a coincidence. Nevertheless, thousands of teenage girls have visited the real J. Dawson's gravesite at Fairview Lawn Cemetery in Nova Scotia, Canada, where 121 of those who lost their lives aboard the *Titanic* are buried. Many visitors have left flowers and ticket stubs from the movie at Dawson's gravesite.

Eventually, the love story and the character of Jack Dawson won DiCaprio over. So did the chance to work with director James Cameron, who was famous for directing big-budget action movies such as *Aliens*, *Terminator*, and *Terminator 2*. DiCaprio thought that he should try doing a big, commercial movie at least once in his career. He notes, "I figured if I was going to work with an action director, James Cameron had to be the one."[34]

As it turns out, DiCaprio was not Cameron's first choice to play the part of Jack. "Leo was recommended by the studios, as were other young hot actors," remembers Cameron. "He didn't strike me as necessarily having the qualities I wanted for my Jack." Cameron's first choices were Matthew McConaughey or Chris O'Donnell. But once Cameron met DiCaprio, he changed his mind: "I basically just loved him. He can quickly charm a group of people without doing anything obvious … the second I met him I was convinced."[35]

Cameron had only one concern about his final casting choice for Jack Dawson—the character was very different from DiCaprio's previous roles. Early on, he pulled DiCaprio aside and said it was important not to portray the character as moody and neurotic, like some of his earlier performances. Cameron explains: "Leo wanted [Jack's character to be] darker, more disturbed. I told him, no, [Jack] is a ray of sunshine. The character lights up the screen and lights up this girl's life."[36]

Titanic Goes Overboard

The story behind the blockbuster movie begins with the sinking of the RMS *Titanic*, one of the worst peacetime maritime disasters in history. Ironically, the ocean liner was billed as "unsinkable" when it was launched on its maiden voyage from Southampton, England, to New York in April 1912. Five days into the voyage, the *Titanic* struck an iceberg some 400 miles (644km) off the coast of Newfoundland. The vessel sank in less than three hours. It was equipped with only enough lifeboats for roughly half the passengers and crew. Of the approximately twenty-two hundred people aboard, more than fifteen hundred perished in the icy waters of the North Atlantic that night.

Director James Cameron, right, sets up a scene with Kate Winslet, left, and DiCaprio on the watery set of Titanic.

The *Titanic* was the largest passenger ship in the world at the time. It was also one of the most luxurious, built at a cost of $7.3 million (a similar ship today would cost hundreds of millions of dollars). There are certain parallels between the ship and the movie; both were big, and both were enormously expensive to make. In fact, *Titanic* was the most expensive movie ever made, at a cost of over $200 million ($125 million over budget). DiCaprio's salary alone was $2.5 million. A new studio was built on the coast of Baja, Mexico, at a cost of $57 million, which included an almost full-size, 750-foot (228.6m) replica of the starboard side of the ship. *Titanic* was such a hugely expensive film that it required financing from two major Hollywood studios—Paramount and Twentieth Century Fox.

Part of the reason the film went so far over its proposed budget was Cameron's perfectionism, which often meant filming the same scene over and over. This caused the filming to take longer than expected, which added an additional $20 million to $30 million to the price tag. In addition, the special effects were very complicated, which also slowed down production.

James Cameron

James Cameron was born in Ontario, Canada, on August 16, 1954. He grew up in a small Canadian town near Niagara Falls. His family moved to Southern California when he was seventeen. Cameron majored in physics at California State University, but after graduation his ambition was to become a screenwriter. He took a job as a truck driver to support himself during this time. His big break came in 1984 when he wrote and directed *The Terminator*, starring Arnold Schwarzenegger. Since then, Cameron has written, directed, or produced several other notable movies, including *Aliens* (1986), *Terminator 2: Judgment Day* (1991), *True Lies* (1994), *Titanic* (1997), and *Avatar* (2009).

James Cameron holds the three Oscar statuettes he was awarded in 1998 for Best Picture, Best Director, and Best Film Editing for Titanic.

Cameron is one of the highest-grossing directors of all time. He is known for making expensive movies that are loaded with special effects. Cameron is also an inventor who is recognized for innovations in underwater cinematography and remote vehicle technologies. He also codeveloped the digital 3-D Fusion Camera System. In July 2009 he announced that *Titanic* would be re-released in 3-D in 2012 for the one hundredth anniversary of the sinking of the ship. In December 2009 Cameron was honored with a star on the Hollywood Walk of Fame.

Titanic took seven grueling months to film, during which time it was heavily promoted. Its highly anticipated release, originally scheduled for July 2, 1997, had to be pushed back four months. The long wait only seemed to generate more interest in the film, with some wondering whether it would live up to the hype or become the most expensive disappointment in cinematic history.

One person who predicted that *Titanic* would be a success when it was released is Tobey Maguire, a fellow actor and one of DiCaprio's closest and oldest friends. "Little does Leo know what's going to happen when *Titanic* comes out," said Maguire. "I mean, it's huge. And it's not going to be just twelve-year-old girls watching him. It's going to be everyone."[37] He could not have been more right.

International Superstar

DiCaprio had dealt with being recognized in public since *Romeo + Juliet*. He learned to deal graciously with the paparazzi and fans who approached him for photographs or an autograph. *Titanic*, however, spun the adoration of DiCaprio out of control and changed his life forever.

When the movie finally premiered at the Tokyo International Film Festival on November 1, 1997, DiCaprio got his first taste of true international superstardom. He arrived in Japan without a single bodyguard and was met at the airport by twenty-five thousand screaming teenage girls. The experience unnerved him. The night of the premiere at the Orchard Hall Theater, the studio provided him with forty-nine security guards. The screaming, chanting crowd mobbed his limousine. One frenzied fan screamed, "Leo, I'm ready to die for you!"[38] The security guards had to rush him through the crowd and whisk him quickly through a side entrance of the theater.

The incident in Tokyo was only a hint of things to come, however. The scene would repeat itself all over the world. Wherever he went he was followed by fans, many of them tearful teenage girls, and chased by paparazzi, who sat waiting for him in six SUVs outside his home in Los Angeles. He was mobbed by photographers and

Fans in Japan crowd for a glimpse of DiCaprio at the 10th Tokyo International Film Festival in 1997, where Titanic made its world premier. The success of Titanic made DiCaprio an international star.

reporters. Crowds of teenage girls chanting his name surrounded him when he appeared in public. They would interrupt him in restaurants to ask for his autograph or on the basketball court to demand pieces of his clothing. It seemed his face was splashed on the cover of every tabloid and magazine at the newsstand, and he was named to *People* magazine's "50 Most Beautiful People in the World" two years running. Even his grandmother in Germany was hounded by his fans; giddy young girls would call her home telephone number repeatedly and ask to speak to Leo. His became one of the most recognizable faces in the world. As he related in a 2010 interview: "I was in the middle of the rainforest in Brazil, where a naked Indian gentleman recognised me from *Titanic*. That was one of the more surreal moments of my life."[39]

"He Never Does Anything But Love You"

The reason for Leo-mania, of course, was the enormous success of *Titanic* itself. It was the number one film for sixteen weeks after it opened. It was the highest grossing movie up to that time and was the first movie ever to gross over a billion dollars. It remained the highest grossing film for twelve years, until 2010, when *Avatar* (2009), also written and directed by Cameron, surpassed it.

Titanic is a long movie (three hours and fourteen minutes); longer, as critics enjoyed pointing out, than it took the ship to sink. The movie's long running time meant that theaters could only show it three times a day, instead of the usual four showings of shorter movies. Many theaters made up the loss in ticket sales by adding midnight screenings, which lasted past three o'clock in the morning. The film almost immediately earned a loyal fan base, and even the midnight showings were routinely sold out. People—mostly teenage girls—saw the movie over and over, taking more friends with them each time. These repeat viewers, some of whom paid to see the movie in theaters dozens of times, were part of the reason the movie took in so much money at the box office.

Columnist Carole Lieberman, a media psychiatrist, has another theory about why *Titanic* sparked Leo-mania: "I think that the mass hysteria and adoration that people feel towards Leonardo in his role in *Titanic* is a combination of who he is—or at least, how he seems on camera—and the role itself."[40] Indeed, many girls and young women viewed the character of Jack Dawson as the ideal romantic hero, a chivalrous young man who was willing to give up his life for the woman he loved. Part of Jack Dawson's—and therefore Leonardo DiCaprio's—enormous mass appeal was that Jack was "this totally devoted boyfriend who then disappears. He never gets old, he never gets dry, he never does anything but love you,"[41] said movie producer Julia Phillips.

Meanwhile, as the worldwide hysteria over him grew, DiCaprio began to feel the toll on his personal life. The degree of attention left him baffled and started to interfere with his ability to enjoy day-to-day life. He began to hide out, locking himself up at home and away from the world. When he did go out, he would

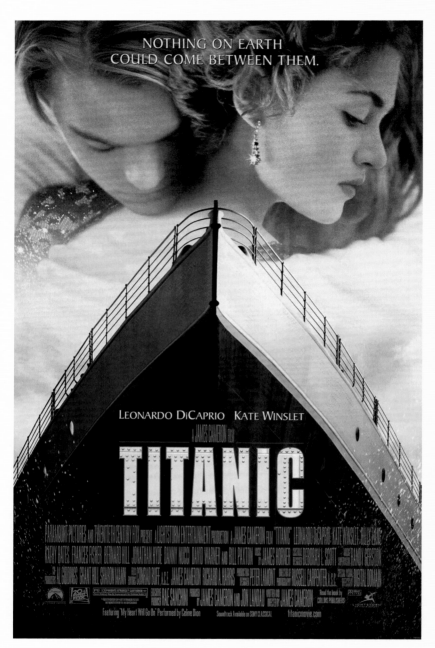

A Titanic promotional poster touts the love story that sparked "Leo-mania," a term the media used to describe the fan frenzy over DiCaprio and his character, Jack Dawson.

hide beneath a blanket on the floor of a friend's car to escape the lenses of the paparazzi. During this crazy time, his four-year-long relationship with Kristen Zang came to an end. He continued to hide out from the public, until his friends finally persuaded him to go out in public and continue doing the things he loved.

Snubbed at the Oscars

Titanic was nominated for eight Golden Globe Awards, including Best Actor, Best Actress, Best Director, and Best Film. In addition, the movie was nominated for a record fourteen Academy Awards, of which it won eleven, including Best Picture and Best Director. Kate Winslet and Gloria Stuart, who played the character of Rose as an old woman, were both nominated for the Oscar. Yet despite the movie's phenomenal success at the box office, which was due in no small part to DiCaprio and his cultlike following, his much-praised performance was not nominated for an Oscar.

Fans display a banner in support of DiCaprio outside of the Shrine Auditorium in Los Angeles before the Academy Award ceremonies in 1998. Many were shocked when DiCaprio was not nominated for an Oscar for his performance in Titanic.

Some people saw this as a deliberate snub of DiCaprio—devoted fans in particular made hundreds of phone calls and sent hundreds of angry e-mails to the Academy of Motion Picture Arts and Sciences. Cameron had his own idea about why DiCaprio was not nominated, saying that the Academy had always been wary of young stars who had achieved too much fame too quickly. When *Titanic* won its eleven Oscars, DiCaprio was not in attendance. Instead, as his mother told reporters, he watched the award show at home on television.

Was *Titanic* the End?

DiCaprio's career and popularity were in overdrive. To the twenty-three-year-old superstar, though, it all felt unreal. As he told a reporter for *Time* magazine: "I have no connection with me during that whole *Titanic* phenomenon and what my face became around the world. ... I'll never reach that state of popularity again, and I don't expect to. It's not something I'm going to try to achieve either."[42] DiCaprio felt that the film's enormous success, and his association with the role of Jack Dawson, made it difficult for audiences to see him in any other role. He may have been right—at least, for a while.

His next film, *The Man in the Iron Mask* (1998), was released on the heels of *Titanic*. The film received mediocre reviews from critics but was a success at the box office, likely because of the enormous drawing power of DiCaprio. In this eighteenth-century tale, loosely based on the novel by Alexandre Dumas, DiCaprio played a dual role, that of Louis XIV, king of France, and Louis's long-imprisoned brother. Ebert said the movie lacked focus and called it "basically just a costume swashbuckler,"[43] though he agreed that the movie was enjoyable and the cast very watchable. For his dual role, however, DiCaprio was awarded a Golden Raspberry Award for Worst Screen Couple. Commonly known as a Razzie, this satirical award is given out yearly to recognize the worst films and performances.

Meanwhile, Leo-mania was still going full steam around the world. DiCaprio says of that time: "It was pretty disheartening

DiCaprio portrays King Louis XIV of France in **The Man in the Iron Mask** *in 1998, his follow up to* **Titanic**.

to be objectified like that. I wanted to stop acting for a little bit. It changed my life in a lot of ways."[44] DiCaprio did take some time off from acting, time spent contemplating life and what he wanted out of it. He traveled the world, goofed around with his friends, and generally blew off steam after the stress of making so many movies one right after another. He also thought a lot about his lifelong concern for the environment and endangered species and ways he could help make the world a better place. He knew that when he returned to acting, it would be to make films that were very different from the love story of *Titanic*.

After a two-year absence from the screen, DiCaprio's next project was the 2000 drama *The Beach*. Because his name still had enormous drawing power, he was paid $20 million for the movie. As a reporter for *Esquire* magazine pointed out: "He's been absent from the screen, presumably hoping the hubbub [over *Titanic*] will wane but instead turning his next project, *The Beach*, into an even bigger deal. He's going to have to be terrific in it for the movie not to come off as a letdown."[45] *The Beach* did well at the box office, grossing $144 million internationally. Critics, however, felt the movie was a disappointment. They complained it did not live up to the potential of its interesting premise about a trio of young tourists who seek paradise on a utopian island near Thailand. His role as a backpacking American earned DiCaprio his second nomination for a Razzie Award.

Moviegoers and critics began to wonder, after the massive success of *Titanic* followed by the letdown of the mediocre films *The Man in the Iron Mask* and *The Beach*, whether DiCaprio had already reached his peak. They had only to wait, however, for his next two films to see that he was capable of following up on the phenomenal success he had achieved at such a young age.

Chapter 4

From Teen Heartthrob to Serious Actor

After *Titanic* and the frenzy of public attention that followed, DiCaprio deliberately chose roles that contrasted with the heroic, romantic Jack Dawson in order to escape the hype and avoid being typecast. In fact, he has often said to directors and fellow actors, "I don't do male leads in love stories any more."[46]

Although *The Man in the Iron Mask* and *The Beach* had both failed to live up to the success of *Titanic*, DiCaprio was undeterred. He continued to pursue roles that interested him and did not worry about the critical reception of his films. He took on more adult roles and focused on becoming a serious, respected dramatic actor, rather than a teen heartthrob. He continued to work with some of the biggest directors and stars in the business, including Martin Scorsese, Steven Spielberg, Tom Hanks, Matt Damon, and Russell Crowe. His skill as an actor was rewarded with two more Academy Award nominations.

His movie roles were not the only thing that matured during this period; his personal life, too, took a serious and dramatic turn. Although he had ended his relationship with Kristen Zang during his hiatus from acting, he soon found another love— Brazilian supermodel Gisele Bündchen. But there was tragedy in his personal life as well, including some violent incidents that left him injured. Incidents such as these, along with his penchant for going to nightclubs, affected his image and earned him a reputation for sometimes reckless behavior.

Leo Makes a Comeback

DiCaprio had taken two years off from acting before appearing in *The Beach*. Following the disappointment of this movie, it would be another two years before he appeared on the screen again. But it was well worth the wait: In 2002 he costarred in two very successful films: *Gangs of New York* and *Catch Me If You Can*. These not only put him in the public eye again, they did much to help revive his career and repair whatever damage to his reputation his previous two films had caused.

Gangs of New York was directed by Martin Scorsese, a legendary figure in the film industry. Scorsese directed *Taxi Driver*, one of DiCaprio's favorite films. DiCaprio had dreamed of working with Scorsese ever since he first watched *Taxi Driver* when he was sixteen. He also wanted to be involved in *Gangs of New York*, an extremely violent movie based on a little-known but true incident that occurred in the Five Points district of New York City in the mid-1800s, when a bloody riot broke out among various immigrant groups in the city. The historical film had been a pet project of Scorsese's for years.

DiCaprio was in Thailand filming *The Beach* when he got word that he had been cast in *Gangs of New York*. DiCaprio recalls what it was like to work with Scorsese at last, as well as how desperate he had been to be involved with the film *Gangs of New York*:

> It was great to collaborate with a director who had been developing a project for twenty-five years. The passion for accuracy in every detail of the period and historical context resonates throughout Marty's work. I heard about the project when I was sixteen—the story of a young Irish immigrant in the 1800s who is placed in the center of the biggest urban riot in the New World. I was so determined to do this project with him that I actually changed agencies when I was seventeen in order to be in closer contact.[47]

In 2002, DiCaprio starred in the critically acclaimed Gangs of New York, *his first collaboration with director Martin Scorsese.*

Martin Scorsese

Martin Scorsese was born on November 17, 1942, in Queens, New York. In 1966 he received a degree in film directing from New York University. He cowrote and directed his breakthrough film, *Mean Streets,* in 1973. Scorsese went on to direct many more notable films, including *Taxi Driver* (1976), *Alice Doesn't Live Here Anymore* (1974), *Raging Bull* (1980), and *The Age of Innocence* (1993). He frequently works with actors on more than one film, including Robert De Niro, Harvey Keitel, Joe Pesci, and most recently, Leonardo DiCaprio. *Gangs of New York* (2002) was the first film Scorsese directed DiCaprio in. Three more collaborations have followed so far: *The Aviator*

Director Martin Scorsese, left, poses with DiCaprio in 2010 to celebrate the premiere of **Shutter Island,** *their fourth movie together.*

(2004), which earned DiCaprio a Golden Globe for Best Actor; *The Departed* (2006); and their most recent film, *Shutter Island* (2010).

Scorsese has earned recognition as one of Hollywood's great film directors. Among his many awards are a Golden Globe for Best Director for *Gangs of New York* and an Academy Award and a Golden Globe for Best Director for *The Departed.* In 1997 he received the American Film Institute Life Achievement Award. In 2007 *Time* magazine put him on its list of the 100 Most Influential People in the World.

The film marked the first truly adult role DiCaprio had taken on. Sian Grigg, who did the makeup for *Gangs of New York*, had literally watched DiCaprio grow up. Grigg explains: "Leo looks so different in this film. He looks more grown up and rugged than I've ever made him look before. The first time I worked with him he was twenty-one, and now he's twenty-six. This is a different role for him—he plays quite a rough character."[48] In one segment of the movie, DiCaprio's character has been badly beaten, necessitating the use of prosthetics to give the appearance of an eye swollen shut. Grigg says this was the first time DiCaprio had to wear prosthetics in a film and recalls that "it wasn't easy for [DiCaprio] to sit still for the three to four hours it took"[49] to prepare for filming the part.

Gangs of New York was nominated for ten Academy Awards, including Best Picture and Best Director. It was released only a few days before *Catch Me If You Can*; both films premiered in December 2002. The themes of the two movies, however, were vastly different. One was filled with gory violence and adult

DiCaprio appears with co-star Tom Hanks and director Steven Spielberg at the premiere of Catch Me If You Can *in 2002.*

themes. The other, while inspired by a true story of a youthful crime spree, was more lighthearted, even amusing at times. In *Catch Me If You Can*, directed by Steven Spielberg, DiCaprio plays Frank Abagnale Jr., a check forger who had successfully impersonated a pilot, a doctor, and a lawyer by his nineteenth birthday. The movie costars Tom Hanks in the role of the FBI agent who pursued and arrested Abagnale. The film enjoyed financial success at the box office, grossing $352 million worldwide, and favorable reviews from critics. Ebert said DiCaprio was "breezy and charming"[50] in the film, particularly in one scene in which he walks into his new classroom at school and promptly—and quite successfully—begins to impersonate a substitute teacher.

Both *Gangs of New York* and *Catch Me If You Can* did well at the box office and with critics. DiCaprio received his third Golden Globe nomination for his portrayal of Abagnale. Despite all the positive reviews, however, his role in *Catch Me If You Can* did not win him the prestigious award. Regardless, it seemed that DiCaprio had managed to put his career back on track. His next three films would bring high accolades to what many were now seeing as a more mature, serious actor.

The Elusive Academy Award

DiCaprio's second collaboration with Martin Scorsese was *The Aviator* (2004). The film stylishly depicts the life and struggles of legendary Howard Hughes, an extremely versatile man who was a filmmaker as well as one of the most influential aviators in American history. Hughes, America's first billionaire and the world's richest man, became increasingly and famously eccentric toward the end of his life. His fear of germs and the outside world drove him to live as a complete recluse. *The Aviator* was a critical and box-office success. It was nominated for numerous awards. For his performance as Hughes, the thirty-year-old DiCaprio won a Golden Globe for Best Actor, his first. The film was also nominated for eleven Academy Awards, including Best Director for Scorsese and Best Actor for DiCaprio. Although this was his second Academy Award

DiCaprio holds his Golden Globe Award for Best Performance by an Actor in a Motion Picture for The Aviator in 2005.

nomination, and there was much speculation in the press that he was certain to win for his intense portrayal of the complicated, neurotic Hughes, the most prestigious of all film awards eluded DiCaprio again. (Jaime Foxx won for the film *Ray*.)

Haven't Seen It?

Leonardo DiCaprio has appeared in dozens of films, but two of his movies have never been shown in U.S. theaters. The first is *The Foot Shooting Party*, filmed in 1994. This short film is about a young man who tries to get out of being sent off to the Vietnam War by having his friends shoot him in the foot. It was made as part of a program for experimental films

DiCaprio and an unidentified co-star appear in a scene from Don's Plum, *a low-budget film from 2001 that was never released in the United States.*

at Touchstone Pictures. *The Foot Shooting Party* was shown at two film festivals but was never released commercially.

Don's Plum was filmed in 2001 and costarred Kevin Connolly and DiCaprio's pal Tobey Maguire. The low-budget, black-and-white film featured mostly improvised dialogue as the actors sit around a table at a diner. DiCaprio appeared in the film as a favor to the director, R.D. Robb, who was another old friend of his. *Don's Plum* was not released in the United States or Canada but did show in Germany. The film led to a falling-out between DiCaprio and the director, who wanted to expand the movie to a full-length film rather than the short film they had all originally agreed to make. DiCaprio felt that the longer version of the film was not as good as the shorter version.

In 2006, DiCaprio appeared in both *Blood Diamond* and *The Departed*. He received his third Academy Award nomination, his second for Best Actor, for *Blood Diamond*. In this film he plays a diamond smuggler from Rhodesia, and he was highly praised for his mastery of a South African accent, a very difficult dialect to imitate. Despite rave reviews of his performance, he was disappointed once again; the Academy Award went to Forest Whitaker for his portrayal of Ugandan dictator Idi Amin in another film set in Africa, *The Last King of Scotland*.

The Departed was the third collaboration between DiCaprio and Scorsese. In this film, DiCaprio plays an undercover cop who must infiltrate the mob. The movie debuted at number one in the box office and earned high praise from critics. *The Departed* won four Academy Awards, including Best Picture and Best Director. DiCaprio's costar Mark Wahlberg was nominated for Best Supporting Actor, but DiCaprio himself was not nominated for his performance.

However, appearing in two such highly acclaimed movies in the same year put DiCaprio in an interesting situation. He was nominated for the Golden Globe for Best Actor for both *Blood Diamond* and *The Departed*, which meant he was up against himself for the award. In this unusual situation, it seemed like a sure thing that he would win a Golden Globe for one role or the other. DiCaprio, however, was to be disappointed again. Like the Oscar, the Golden Globe went to Whitaker. The string of losses led many fans to wonder if DiCaprio would ever win the highly acclaimed acting awards they believed he deserved.

Rumors of Romance

DiCaprio's career seemed solid at this point, with three Academy Award nominations under his belt. He had earned respect as an adult actor and was often referred to by directors, fellow actors, and the media as the best actor of his generation. Meanwhile, however, his name was often in the press for reasons other than his acting career.

The intense media scrutiny that began after *Romeo + Juliet* and *Titanic* continued to expose and put pressure on his private life.

DiCaprio poses with then girlfriend Gisele Bündchen before the start of the Academy Awards ceremony in 2005.

DiCaprio's name was linked in the press with a growing list of actresses and models, something that had not changed from the beginning of his career. During the filming of *Gangs of New York*, for example, there were rumors that he and Cameron Diaz were romantically involved. Despite the speculation in the press, the two young actors, who had been friends for several years, never advanced beyond friendship. Most of the other affairs he was purportedly involved in were also mere rumors.

In fact, DiCaprio had been in a relationship with Brazilian supermodel Gisele Bündchen since 2001. They dated off and on for several years. During one breakup Bündchen moved back to Brazil for eight months to nurse her hurt feelings. At one point they were briefly engaged. Amid gossip in the tabloids that DiCaprio and Bündchen were planning their wedding, the two split up for good in 2005. Later that same year, DiCaprio began another long-term, on-again off-again relationship, this time with Israeli model Bar Refaeli. Even so, the press continues to speculate about his relationships with other women, including most of the actresses who have appeared in films with him.

A Close Call

In addition to the constant attention the tabloids paid to his romantic life, DiCaprio was also in the news for some violent incidents in his personal life. He had long ago earned a reputation as a hard partier, owing to his fondness for heavy drinking and club hopping. In fact, there were rumors going back to his days filming *The Basketball Diaries* that he was using drugs in real life—rumors he continues to deny today. Yet his partying behavior not only caused the press to speculate that he was heading down the wrong path, it also led to an incident that would plague him for several years.

In a lawsuit that went on until 2004, onetime actor Roger Wilson sued DiCaprio for allegedly encouraging two of his friends to attack Wilson outside a Manhattan restaurant in May 1998. The incident revolved around the actress Elizabeth Berkley, who was Wilson's girlfriend at the time. In the $45 million lawsuit,

Wilson claimed that DiCaprio had told his buddies to go outside and beat him up. In September 2004, a judge dropped the charges against DiCaprio. Paul Callan, DiCaprio's lawyer, said, "It's an exceptionally long and old case. … For Leonardo DiCaprio, it was an entirely frivolous lawsuit. … He was named because he is a prominent celebrity."[51] Although the case against him was dismissed and DiCaprio said he felt "total vindication,"[52] this serious incident nevertheless put his name in a bad light.

Although the lawsuit that had dragged on for more than five years was dismissed, more violence erupted in DiCaprio's personal life in 2005. While on a short break in the filming of *The Departed*, DiCaprio attended a Hollywood party given by an ex-boyfriend of Paris Hilton. During the party, a woman who was trespassing and had been asked to leave the property came across DiCaprio outside, where she assaulted him with a broken beer bottle, slashing his face and neck. He was rushed to the hospital, where he needed twelve stitches to close the gashes. Doctors said he would need plastic surgery to repair the damage. Moreover, the wound could have been fatal because the bottle had struck dangerously close to his jugular vein. An unidentified friend of the actor said afterward, "Leo's really shaken up and he's worried about how his wound will heal. His face is his fortune and it would be devastating for him to be left with an ugly scar. He'll have to have plastic surgery. But, he realises he's lucky to have escaped with his life."[53]

DiCaprio knows he was lucky that night. He also knows just how lucky he has been in his career. Not many child actors have been able to make the transition to adult roles as successfully as he has. More than luck, though, his talent and hard work have brought him to where he is today—a successful and well-respected dramatic actor who can call his own shots.

Chapter 5

Off-Camera Causes

DiCaprio is involved in a number of humanitarian and environmental causes that are very dear to his heart. In fact, he has made almost as big a name for himself as an environmentalist as he has as an actor. On his Twitter page, for example, he bills himself as "Actor, Environmentalist and Philanthropist,"[54] a sign of how much a part of his identity he feels his off-camera causes are. DiCaprio has been highly praised for his charitable efforts and has even won several awards for his environmental work. In spite of this recognition, he has always been very modest about his activism. Unlike some celebrity do-gooders, his motives have little to do with publicity or self-image. His desire to make the world a better place is rooted in something much deeper.

Family Influence

DiCaprio's family history, childhood experiences, and compassion for those less fortunate than himself have all motivated his interest in charitable causes. Although now he is, as one reporter put it, "rich, rich, rich thanks to *Titanic* and a slew of other hits,"[55] DiCaprio grew up poor, an experience that had a lasting effect on him. He knows firsthand what it means to have to do without and to struggle to get by.

His parents' influence has also contributed to his charitable nature. His father was a peace activist in the 1960s during the Vietnam War. He often spoke to his son about the importance of working to make the world a better place. His mother was born in Germany during World War II, and she and her parents

Charity for the Last *Titanic* Survivor

DiCaprio has used part of his income from the movie *Titanic* to help a real-life survivor of the catastrophe: Millvina Dean. Dean was only an infant when the ship went down in the frigid waters of the North Atlantic in 1912. Her father died that night, but Dean, her older brother, and her mother survived. Over the course of her life, Dean participated in many events related to the *Titanic*, including conventions, exhibitions, interviews, and documentaries.

Millvina Dean, the last living Titanic survivor, received financial support from DiCaprio and Kate Winslet during her final years until her death in 2009.

By 2006 Dean was living in a nursing home and her health began to fail. In 2008, a broken hip forced her to auction off many family possessions and personal mementos associated with the *Titanic* to pay her medical costs. A fund was set up jointly by the Belfast, British, and International Titanic Societies in April 2009 to help support Dean. DiCaprio donated $20,000 to this fund, which helped pay for Dean's room in the nursing home as well as her medical costs (Kate Winslet did the same). Dean died of pneumonia at age ninety-seven on May 31, 2009. Her ashes were scattered from the dock in Southampton, England, where the ship set sail.

suffered the deprivations and hardships of the war. DiCaprio grew up hearing about the injustice and horrors of two wars, of people being persecuted and refugees being displaced. The stories he heard as a child still haunt him and have significantly influenced his views about alleviating the suffering of others. DiCaprio gives his parents credit for his interest in humanitarian and environmental causes, and for shaping his worldview. Their influence and involvement in his life is something that continues even today, and he thanks them for making him the philanthropic person he is.

DiCaprio's interest in the environment began as a young child, when he would watch documentaries on the rain forest and endangered animals. This interest has lasted throughout his life. "I admit I don't walk to work and I don't have a compost pile," he said in a 2010 interview, "but I am trying to set an example."[56]

Working to Fight Global Warming

One environmental cause DiCaprio is particularly committed to is global warming. In 1998, he formed the Leonardo DiCaprio Foundation to raise awareness of several environmental issues, especially climate change. The foundation stresses the importance of using alternative and renewable energy sources instead of oil and other fossil fuels, which are believed to contribute to global warming. In 2008, his foundation joined with the California Community Foundation and is now known as the Leonardo DiCaprio Fund at CCF, which continues to support environmental causes.

DiCaprio practices what he preaches in his daily life. For example, whenever possible, he travels by commercial airline rather than private jet in order not to waste fuel. He concedes, however, that "there are situations within my industry where I have to get to someplace during a time frame where it's impossible to fly commercial. Otherwise, I demand that I do fly commercial. Not to mention the fact that if there were a hybrid private plane, I would be on it."[57] In addition, he has owned several different hybrid vehicles, including a Toyota Prius, a BMW hydrogen car,

DiCaprio, an advocate for environmental issues, speaks about global warming on behalf of the National Resources Defense Council (NRDC) in 2003.

and a Lexus hybrid sedan, his current car. He has an apartment in Riverhouse, an eco-friendly building in Manhattan, and owns a so-called smart home in Los Angeles that uses solar panels.

Most recently, DiCaprio lobbied for the use of solar panels on the set of his futurist mystery film *Inception*. He explained in an interview:

> A lot of this movie (*Inception*) was made with solar power. It's the first movie I got to do with solar power. I had a conversation about it with Alan Horn, who's the head of Warner Bros. The generators that we had on the set were all powered by solar energy. It's going to be a big conversion to do stuff like that every day, not just in making movies but everything in the world.[58]

DiCaprio's commitment to environmentalism and renewable energy extends to other areas of his life, as well. He bought part of a 104-acre (42ha) island off the coast of Belize in 2005 and began plans to open an eco-friendly resort there. When completed, the resort will feature an eighty-room hotel, several smaller condominiums and private villas, and eco-tours of the tropical island and the nearby barrier reef. The buildings and tours are designed to minimize the impact of the ecotourism and to respect the island's natural environment. Most importantly to DiCaprio, the resort will be "green"—powered by renewable energy sources.

Environmental Projects and Honors

In 2007 DiCaprio cowrote, coproduced, and narrated the documentary *The 11th Hour*, which focuses on the environmental consequences of global warming. To prepare for making his documentary, he spent several hours one day talking about the impact of climate change on the environment with former vice president Al Gore, who narrated the internationally known documentary on global warming *An Inconvenient Truth*. *The 11th Hour* did poorly at the box office and drew equally disappointing reviews—in fact, one critic called it "mind-numbingly dull" and "grindingly boring."[59] Only three weeks after it was released, the documentary was pulled from theaters and put on DVD.

Despite the lukewarm reception of *The 11th Hour*, DiCaprio remains undeterred in his commitment to saving the planet. He has narrated two other films concerning the environment, both of which are available for viewing on his website. In *Water Planet* he explains, "Water is a finite substance, a limited resource.... Water is being threatened by pollution. ... So many chemicals flow into rivers and lakes that the actual composition of water in some places has been fundamentally changed."[60] In *Global Warming*, he warns that because of human activities, particularly the burning of fossil fuels, "We are altering life on this planet as we know it."[61]

DiCaprio has been both praised and honored for his environmental efforts. In 2000, for example, he was invited to chair the annual Earth Day commemoration and appeared in Washington, D.C., for the event. This honor prompted him to write an article titled "Get Wise to Global Warming" that appeared in *Time*

DiCaprio signs his name to a petition from Global Green USA in 2005 asking world leaders to ensure their citizens have access to clean water. Global Green awarded him its Environmental Leadership Award in 2003.

magazine. DiCaprio's activism also earned him an Environmental Leadership Award from Global Green in 2003. Global Green, the American arm of Green Cross International, works to fight global climate change. (His mother was given the same award from Global Green in 2007.) During the 2007 Academy Awards show, he and fellow presenter Al Gore announced that the show had incorporated

Leo Talks About Eating Beef

Leonardo DiCaprio eats meat, but it is a lifestyle choice he has mixed feelings about. During an interview for *Time* magazine in 2000, for example, DiCaprio ordered a hamburger for lunch. Later, when the reporter got up to make a phone call, DiCaprio grabbed the microphone and snuck the following message onto the reporter's tape recorder:

> I shouldn't be eating hamburgers, because the methane gas cows release is the No. 1 contributor to the destruction of the ozone layer; and the No. 1 reason they destroy the rain forest is to make grazing ground for cattle. So it's very ironic that I eat beef, being the environmentalist that I am. But then again, if I ordered the tuna sandwich, I would be promoting the fact that they have large tuna nets that capture innocent little dolphins.

Quoted in Joel Stein, "Cinema: What's Eating Leonardo DiCaprio?" *Time*, February 21, 2000. www.time.com/time/magazine/article/0,9171,996132-4,00.html.

environmentally friendly practices in its planning and production. And in 2007, DiCaprio was one of the presenters at the very first Live Earth. This is an annual music event, cofounded by former vice president Al Gore, that works to combat global climate change. In 2008 DiCaprio was further honored when he was invited to speak before the Scottish parliament on global warming.

Saving Endangered Species

DiCaprio is also passionate about saving endangered species from extinction. One example is the tiger. There are only an estimated 3,200 tigers left in the wild. In 2010, the Chinese Year of the Tiger, DiCaprio teamed up with the World Wildlife Fund to form Save

Tigers Now. This campaign will travel to remote parts of Asia to study tigers in the wild and examine possible strategies for saving the animal from extinction. DiCaprio explains the importance of the campaign: "Tigers are endangered and critical to some of the world's most important ecosystems. Key conservation efforts can save the tiger species from extinction, protect some of the planet's last wild habitats and help sustain the local communities surrounding them. By protecting this iconic species, we can save so much more."[62] The goal of Save Tigers Now is to double the wild tiger population by 2022, the next Year of the Tiger.

Another species DiCaprio has worked to protect is the critically endangered mountain gorilla. In 2008, he wrote the afterword to the book *Breakfast in the Rainforest*, which details the plight of this majestic creature. As DiCaprio writes:

> For ages, gorillas have fascinated us, perhaps because they are very much like us, with more than 95 percent of their DNA identical to ours. Gorillas are the largest of the primates and live in the beautiful forested mountains of central Africa. Sadly, today, mountain gorillas are threatened by extinction due to human activities. There are only 650 of these remarkable creatures left in the world. What a tragedy it would be to lose these creatures that are so close to us.[63]

Helping His Neighbors in Need

DiCaprio has other off-camera causes that stem from his desire to help make the world a better place. His charitable nature is evidenced by numerous generous acts. For example, in 1998 he and his mother donated $35,000 to help fund a brand-new computer center at the Los Feliz branch of the Los Angeles Public Library. The building is on the site of his former home and was rebuilt after being destroyed by an earthquake in 1994. He has also performed many acts of kindness for disadvantaged kids, such as donating food and clothing to homeless charities, visiting sick children at the Ronald McDonald House, and donating money to help children who have lost a loved one to AIDS.

Indeed, DiCaprio is especially devoted to helping children in need. While filming *Blood Diamond* in Africa, he worked with twenty-four children from a local orphanage who were extras in the movie, and he was deeply touched by their situation. Some of them had lost relatives and their own limbs because of the harsh practices of the diamond trade. These child amputees were in need of prosthetic limbs, so DiCaprio and other members of the cast and crew set up the Blood Diamond Fund to help care for them and others living in the communities in which the movie was filmed. DiCaprio became particularly fond of one

DiCaprio was one of many celebrities to answer telephones and greet donors at the Hope for Haiti Now: A Global Benefit for Earthquake Relief *telethon in 2010.*

little orphan girl he met at an orphanage in South Africa and is personally sponsoring her. He sends a check each month to help support her and keeps in touch with her by telephone.

DiCaprio's philanthropic nature was further stirred by the devastating earthquake that struck Haiti in January 2010. The earthquake measured 7.0 on the Richter scale and killed 230,000, wounded 300,000, and left 1 million Haitians homeless. DiCaprio donated $1 million to the Clinton Bush Haiti Fund to help meet the immediate and future needs of the Haitian refugees. Former president George W. Bush said: "I salute Leonardo DiCaprio for his extraordinary generosity. This donation sends a clear message to the people of Haiti that America's commitment to helping rebuild their country is strong. I thank Leo for setting a wonderful example for all Americans of helping a neighbor in need."[64]

Leo Takes a Stand

Just as he is not shy about speaking out about causes he believes in, DiCaprio is also quick to voice his political opinions. During the 2000 election, he supported Al Gore, whose concern for global environmental issues DiCaprio shares. While campaigning for John Kerry during the 2004 presidential election, DiCaprio traveled around the country and delivered numerous speeches criticizing the Bush administration's track record on the environment. And in 2008, he donated twenty-three hundred dollars—the maximum amount allowed—to Barack Obama's presidential campaign.

In 2000 he took another stand by founding and maintaining a website called LeonardoDiCaprio.org. The site is devoted to providing timely information about the environment, renewable energy, and endangered species. It links to environmental campaigns DiCaprio supports, such as those which seek to eliminate plastic water bottles and plastic shopping bags, as well as to other environmental websites such as Mother Nature Network and Treehugger. DiCaprio's site also features books and movies that deal with the issues he cares so passionately about.

All of DiCaprio's efforts to help the environment and those who are less fortunate than himself have earned him recognition

DiCaprio speaks at a rally in Iowa on behalf of Democratic presidential candidate John Kerry and his running mate John Edwards during the 2004 campaign.

and respect around the world. That is something for which he is very grateful. As he told an interviewer in 2009, "What I want is to be known as someone who stood for something."[65] That the world knows Leonardo DiCaprio as more than just a movie star is very important to him.

Chapter 6

Leo Today, Leo Tomorrow

Leonardo DiCaprio keeps busy acting in and producing movies, as well as with multiple charitable causes. His face—and his name—are recognized the world over for his work both on camera and off. He appeared in two feature films that were released in 2010, both of which did very well at the box office and prompted talk of another possible Academy Award nomination. As always, he has upcoming movie projects that will keep him busy for several years. His personal life, too, seems to have stabilized, as he and Bar Refaeli rekindled their relationship in early 2010 after a lengthy hiatus. What the long-term future holds for this dynamic young man is unclear, but one thing is certain—he will continue to live his life according to his own terms.

A Bustling Career

In 2010 DiCaprio narrated another documentary on a subject of interest to him—this time, space exploration. This film, *Hubble 3D IMAX*, was made in cooperation with NASA, the U.S. space agency. It focuses on a 2009 mission to repair the Hubble Space Telescope. Toni Myers, the director, said of DiCaprio: "It was wonderful to work with him. He's a very, very hard worker, very dedicated, and he brings a shared sense of awe that we all have about what he's seeing and experiencing."[66] The documentary received favorable reviews for its breathtaking shots of outer space as well as Earth from afar.

DiCaprio pauses outside of the premier of **Shutter Island** *in New York in 2010.*

DiCaprio also appeared in two feature films released in 2010. The first of these, *Shutter Island* (2010), is the fourth film to pair him with director Martin Scorsese. DiCaprio plays a federal agent in the 1950s who is investigating a disappearance from a prison

Turning Books and Real People into Movies

Many of DiCaprio's movies have been either adapted from novels or plays or based on real-life incidents. *Titanic* (1997) and *Gangs of New York* (2002), for example, are based on historical events. Among his films in which he portrays actual people are *Total Eclipse* (1995), about nineteenth-century French poet Arthur Rimbaud, and *The Aviator* (2004), which depicts twentieth-century filmmaker, inventor, and recluse Howard Hughes. *This Boy's Life* (1993), *Basketball Diaries* (1995), and *Catch Me If You Can* (2002) are all based on autobiographies. *Marvin's Room* (1996) was an off-Broadway play, and *Romeo + Juliet* (1996) is an adaptation of the famous play by Shakespeare. Other DiCaprio movies that have come from novels include *What's Eating Gilbert Grape?* (1993), *The Man in the Iron Mask* (1998), *The Beach* (2000), *Body of Lies* (2008), *Revolutionary Road* (2008), and *Shutter Island* (2010).

DiCaprio starred as Howard Hughes in The Aviator *in 2005, one of several real-life people he has portrayed in his films.*

for the criminally insane. This psychological thriller was praised for its surprise ending. It is just the sort of film that DiCaprio most enjoys making. As he told Roger Ebert, "I love the challenge of being able to take on characters that aren't always what they seem."[67] The movie did well at the box office, opening at number one, and went on to become one of Scorsese's highest-grossing films ever. Critics gave it generally positive reviews, although one *New York Times* reviewer warned, "Something terrible is afoot. Sadly, that something turns out to be the movie itself."[68]

The second film starring DiCaprio released in 2010 was *Inception*, released in July, and directed by Christopher Nolan. This was the first science fiction film DiCaprio has attempted. Like *Shutter Island*, it was the number one movie when it opened, taking in just over $60 million on its first weekend of theatrical release. It remained the number one movie three weeks after its release, as well. Critics had mixed feelings about its complicated plot, which contains so many twists and turns that apparently some moviegoers had to see it more than once in order to understand it. A reviewer for *USA Today*, however, liked the fact that the movie was so complex, saying, "It's refreshing to find a director who makes us stretch, even occasionally struggle, to keep up."[69]

The Appian Way

DiCaprio founded his own production company, Appian Way Productions, in 2004. The first films the company was involved with were *The Aviator* and *The Assassination of Richard Nixon* (2004). DiCaprio served as executive producer for both of these films. He has also served as producer or coproducer on a number of other films through his production company, including *Gardener of Eden* (2007), directed by his old friend Kevin Connolly; the horror picture *Orphan* (2009); *Public Enemies* (2009), which starred his old friend Johnny Depp as 1930s American gangster John Dillinger; and *Shutter Island*. DiCaprio even ventured back into TV with the reality series *Greensburg*, which chronicles the rebuilding of the town Greensburg, Kansas, as an environmentally sustainable town after it was hit by a tornado in 2007.

Evidence of DiCaprio's continually healthy career are the dozens of other projects he has on deck in both on-camera and off-camera roles. He served as producer for a number of films that were scheduled for release in 2011, including *Red Riding Hood*, *Atari*, *The Chancellor Manuscript*, *Ninja Scroll*, and *The Low Dweller*. Scheduled

A sign shows the commitment of tornado-ravaged Greensburg, Kansas, to rebuild as an environmentally sustainable town. DiCaprio's production company was involved in a reality series in 2007 documenting the town's progress.

for release in 2012 is *Hoover*, in which DiCaprio will play FBI director J. Edgar Hoover. In addition, DiCaprio has as many as twenty-two other films in various stages of planning and development.

An Uncertain Personal Future

However, the future of DiCaprio's personal life seems somewhat less certain than that of his professional life. After filming *Shutter Island* and *Inception*, he took another of his long breaks from acting. He had several reasons for wanting to take some time off. He was tired after playing two demanding roles back-to-back and simply wanted some time for himself. He was also reflecting on his age—he had just turned thirty-five—and on what he wanted to do next with his life. He says, "I've taken a lot of things seriously, maybe too seriously at times, so I'm going to make sure that whatever I do next and whatever choices I make are really right for me."[70] For now, he is not sure where his life will take him next or which of his many projects he will decide to work on next.

In his romantic life, as well, he remains noncommittal. Since 2005 he has been in an on-again off-again relationship with Israeli model Bar Refaeli, who appeared on the cover of the 2009 *Sports Illustrated* swimsuit edition. As with every woman DiCaprio has been involved with, the press has wildly speculated about whether the two of them would begin living together or even marry. The pair took a six-month break from their relationship but reunited in early 2010, and immediately there were rumors that they had gotten engaged. Both denied the rumors, although Refaeli said that the time apart had made their relationship stronger. More recently, in August 2010, the *Daily Star* gossiped that DiCaprio was planning to propose and had taken his mother with him to shop for an engagement ring.

DiCaprio is accompanied by girlfriend Bar Refaeli at a gala at the International Film Festival Berlinale in Germany in 2010.

Leonardo's Stalker

Leonardo DiCaprio is one of the most highly publicized and recognizable figures in Hollywood, and he has had more than his share of admiring fans approach him for an autograph or a photograph with him. One woman, however, has taken things too far. In August 2010, DiCaprio filed for and was granted a temporary restraining order against a deranged woman who has allegedly been stalking him for several years. Forty-one-year-old Livia Bistriceanu claims that she and DiCaprio are married and that she is carrying his child, whom she has named Jesus. In documents DiCaprio filed in Los Angeles Superior Court, he says Bistriceanu e-mails him constantly, knows where he lives, and has tried to make physical contact with him. DiCaprio says he fears for his own safety as well as the safety of friends and family, because the woman seems to be completely out of touch with reality and appears to have no regard for the consequences of her actions. The restraining order mandates that Bistriceanu stay at least 100 yards (91.44m) away from DiCaprio.

Whether these rumors turn out to be true remains to be seen. DiCaprio has never liked to discuss his romantic life during interviews and prefers not to be asked personal questions about someone he is dating. He did, however, tell a *Rolling Stone* interviewer in the summer of 2010 that he will not feel he has truly grown up until he is married and has children. "That's going to come, it's just a matter of when and how," he assured the interviewer. "Some of my friends have two children and their life has changed. That's going to be the giant leap."[71]

Living Life to Its Fullest

Until he marries and has children, however, DiCaprio will continue to enjoy his bachelor lifestyle. This often finds him on vacations in Europe or visiting other spots around the world. He loves to travel and tends to head for areas where the environment or a particular species is being threatened. His most recent trips have taken him to Bhutan, the Galapagos Islands, the Philippines, and Nepal, where he spent a week and a half in the Himalayas. He especially enjoys visiting places known for their wildlife or natural beauty, which has been a dream of his since childhood.

DiCaprio, a big basketball fan, and Zac Efron, left, sit courtside at a game between the Los Angeles Lakers and the Denver Nuggets in 2008.

He also likes to hang out with his buddies, either at home or out doing a variety of activities. He still enjoys going to nightclubs, although he has toned down his behavior from the wild days of his twenties. He also likes going sailing and scuba diving. His favorite pastime, however, is watching basketball games, especially his favorite team, the LA Lakers. He is often photographed at basketball games with Refaeli or with his pals, including actors Kevin Bacon, Zac Efron, and Kevin Connolly. His other longtime friends include fellow performers Tobey Maguire, Mark Wahlberg, and Lukas Haas. Another old friend is Kate Winslet, to whom he lent a great deal of moral support during her 2010 divorce from director Sam Mendes.

DiCaprio also has a daredevil side to him, and he gets his adrenaline pumping with heart-racing activities such as bungee jumping and skydiving. In fact, DiCaprio has learned firsthand why these are considered extremely high-risk activities. In 1996, DiCaprio and several friends went skydiving in California, jumping from an airplane at 12,000 feet (3,658m). When DiCaprio pulled his rip cord, however, his parachute did not open. Luckily, he was skydiving tandem, which meant he had an instructor with him during the jump. As the two of them continued to fall for twenty-three seconds, DiCaprio's instructor cut away the parachute with a Swiss Army knife and pulled the cord on DiCaprio's emergency chute.

The experience shook him up, but did not stop him from skydiving again. Incredibly, DiCaprio experienced a second jump in which his parachute did not open. After these two harrowing experiences, he realized that he was taking risks with his life just to get a thrill. As he told an interviewer for *Esquire* magazine in 2010:

It's all part of that process of doing things that are daring to be accepted by your peers—and it's absolutely insane. You can enter a never-ending vapid hole trying to catch the next exciting moment without ever stopping to appreciate it. It can be a never-ending process of chasing something that isn't there. I know it's a cliché, but I'm happy to be alive. I went skydiving and my chutes didn't open. Two of them.[72]

These two close calls did not stop him from dabbling in other risky forms of recreation, however. On one trip to the Galapagos

Islands, while scuba diving during an ecotour, he had another mishap that could have turned deadly. While trying to film a school of stingrays underwater, he suddenly realized that his oxygen tanks were not functioning properly and were almost empty. He was too far underwater to be able to surface quickly enough to save himself without getting "the bends," a painful condition caused by a diver rising too quickly to the surface, which releases nitrogen gas in the blood. He recalls, "All you can think about at the moment is, like, 'Get me the hell out of this situation.'"[73] He took one last breath from his tank and propelled himself through the water to where his friends were. They took turns handing him their breathing masks to share their oxygen with him as they all surfaced slowly together to safety.

Once again, though, DiCaprio was not about to give up his favorite activities just because they might put him in danger. He explains, "It makes you feel excited all over again to be alive. I'd hate to die. I try to assess as many different ways as possible not to die. To limit the things that would put me in those predicaments. But there's no way to control any of it, because accidents happen."[74]

"Not Bad for a Kid from East Hollywood"

Robert De Niro said something to a young Leo DiCaprio during the filming of *This Boy's Life* that has stuck with DiCaprio ever since. DiCaprio recalls that during some of the movie's most physically grueling scenes, De Niro said to him, "Look, I know this may suck right now, but pain is temporary, film is forever."[75] DiCaprio says this mantra has stuck with him through the years, and today he still reminds himself that no matter how difficult a shoot is, the images he creates on-screen will be a testament to his hard work and creativity forever.

DiCaprio has clearly taken De Niro's advice to heart, having appeared in nearly thirty movies in the twenty years he has been in the business. He is known as one of the most dedicated and hardest-working actors in the industry. This dedication to film is a part of who he is. He explains his feelings about movies and about acting:

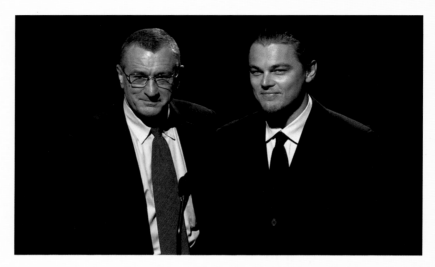

DiCaprio credits Robert De Niro, left, with providing good career advice that has helped him manage difficult film projects.

"I love it. There's no other art form in the world that affects me more. There's nothing that I walk away from feeling transformed by the way I do with cinema. There's something so gratifying about being burned into celluloid and knowing that I can look back later in life and have stories about those experiences. It's an amazing gift."[76]

Early in his career, DiCaprio worried that he would not amount to anything in the film industry. He once admitted, "I thought that on my gravestone they were going to write, 'This is the guy from *Growing Pains*.'"[77] Clearly, he has come a long way from his TV sitcom days. Christopher Nolan, who directed *Inception*, is among those who believe DiCaprio will continue to be a successful actor in the future. Nolan says, "He has that timeless quality about him, like a Jack Nicholson or an Al Pacino. He's going to be a movie star forever."[78] DiCaprio remains very humble about the praise and recognition he receives around the world. He continues to feel lucky simply for having broken into the business. Ultimately, he is grateful to be given the chance to do something he loves. "At the end of the day I know I've had more fun being famous than I would have had otherwise," he says. "The attention I'm getting, having people I respect admire me—it's not bad for a kid from East Hollywood!"[79]

Introduction: The Kid from the Wrong Side of the Tracks

1. Quoted in Nancy Krulik, *Leonardo DiCaprio: A Biography*. New York: Pocket, 1998, p. 50.
2. Quoted in Dotson Rader, "Leonardo DiCaprio, Hollywood Outsider," *Sunday Times* (London), January 11, 2009. http://entertainment.timesonline.co.uk/tol/arts_and_entertainment/film/article5467287.ece.
3. Quoted in Anne-Marie O'Neill, "Riding the Wave," *People*, January 26, 1998. www.people.com/people/archive/article/0,,20124329,00.html.

Chapter 1: A Born Actor

4. Quoted in Krulik, *Leonardo DiCaprio*, p. 5.
5. Quoted in Rader, "Leonardo DiCaprio, Hollywood Outsider."
6. Quoted in O'Neill, "Riding the Wave."
7. Quoted in Rader, "Leonardo DiCaprio, Hollywood Outsider."
8. Quoted in Brian J. Robb, *The Leonardo DiCaprio Album*. London: Plexus, 1998, p. 13.
9. Quoted in O'Neill, "Riding the Wave."
10. Quoted in Kieran Scott, *Leonardo DiCaprio*. New York: Aladdin, 1997, p. 9.
11. Quoted in Robb, *The Leonardo DiCaprio Album*, p. 19.
12. Quoted in Rader, "Leonardo DiCaprio, Hollywood Outsider."
13. Quoted in Sean Smith and David Ansen, "Hollywood Royalty," *Newsweek*, January 29, 2007. www.msnbc.msn.com/id/16720751/site/newsweek.

Chapter 2: Playing the Troubled Teen

14. Quoted in Robb, *The Leonardo DiCaprio Album*, p. 27.
15. Brian Hiatt, "Leo Faces His Demons," *Rolling Stone,* August 5, 2010, p. 50.

16. Quoted in Krulik, *Leonardo DiCaprio*, p. 14.
17. Quoted in Smith and Ansen, "Hollywood Royalty."
18. Quoted in Douglas Thompson, *Leonardo DiCaprio*. New York: Berkeley Boulevard Books, 1998, p. 24.
19. Quoted in Krulik, *Leonardo DiCaprio*, p. 20.
20. Roger Ebert, "This Boy's Life," *Chicago Sun-Times*, April 23, 1993. http://rogerebert.suntimes.com/apps/pbcs.dll/article?AID=/19930423/REVIEWS/304230305/1023.
21. Quoted in Robb, *The Leonardo DiCaprio Album*, p. 32.
22. Quoted in James Cameron-Wilson and F. Maurice Speed, *Film Review, 1994–5*. London: Virgin, 1994, p. 148.
23. Quoted in Cal Fussman, "How Do You Become Leo DiCaprio?" *Esquire*, February 26, 2010. www.esquire.com/features/leonardo-dicaprio-quotes-0310?click=main_sr#ixzz0v6Saxphz.
24. David Ansen, "'Tis Not a Jolly Season," *Newsweek*, December 27, 1993. www.newsweek.com/1993/12/26/tis-not-a-jolly-season.html.
25. Quoted in *Entertainment Weekly*, "Hollywood's 'It' Boy," March 24, 1995. www.ew.com/ew/article/0,,296524,00.html.
26. Edward Guthmann, "DiCaprio's Risky Acting Scores in 'Basketball Diaries,'" *San Francisco Chronicle*, April 21, 1995. www.sfgate.com/cgi-bin/article.cgi?f=/c/a/1995/04/21/DD13160.DTL.
27. Quoted in Robb, *The Leonardo DiCaprio Album*, p. 57.
28. Quoted in Martin Noble, *Leonardo DiCaprio: An Unofficial Biography*. Woodbridge, England: Funfax, 1998, p. 27.
29. Roger Ebert, "Romeo & Juliet," *Chicago Sun-Times*, November 1, 1996. http://rogerebert.suntimes.com/apps/pbcs.dll/article?AID=/19961101/REVIEWS/611010304.
30. Quoted in Robb, *The Leonardo DiCaprio Album*, p. 80.

Chapter 3: Leo-Mania

31. Quoted in Thompson, *Leonardo DiCaprio*, p. 30.
32. Quoted in Noble, *Leonardo DiCaprio*, p. 34.
33. Quoted in Robb, *The Leonardo DiCaprio Album*, p. 88.
34. Quoted in Krulik, *Leonardo DiCaprio*, p. 31.
35. Quoted in Noble, *Leonardo DiCaprio*, p. 32.
36. Quoted in Noble, *Leonardo DiCaprio*, p. 34.
37. Quoted in Scott, *Leonardo DiCaprio*, p. 27.

38. Quoted in O'Neill, "Riding the Wave."
39. Quoted in James Mottram, "Leonardo DiCaprio on Saving the World, Both on and off the Screen," *Herald* (Scotland), July 5, 2010. www.heraldscotland.com/arts-ents/film-tv-features/leonardo-dicaprio-on-saving-the-world-both-on-and-off-the-screen-1.1039309.
40. Quoted in *Portrait of Leonardo: The Kid Who Took Hollywood*, DVD, directed by Christopher Case. Hollywood, CA: Passport International Productions, 1998.
41. Quoted in *Portrait of Leonardo*.
42. Quoted in Joel Stein, "What's Eating Leonardo DiCaprio?" *Time*, February 21, 2000. www.time.com/time/asia/magazine/2000/0221/cover1.html.
43. Roger Ebert, "The Man in the Iron Mask," *Chicago Sun-Times*, March 13, 1998. http://rogerebert.suntimes.com/apps/pbcs.dll/article?AID=/19980313/REVIEWS/803130303.
44. Quoted in Smith and Ansen, "Hollywood Royalty."
45. Tom Carson, "The Esquire 21: Leonardo DiCaprio," *Esquire*, November 1, 1999. www.esquire.com/features/twenty-one-leonardo-dicaprio-1199?click=main_sr#ixzz0v6QKukJX.

Chapter 4: From Teen Heartthrob to Serious Actor

46. Quoted in Mottram, "Leonardo DiCaprio on Saving the World, Both on and off the Screen."
47. Quoted in Miramax Books, *Gangs of New York: Making the Movie*. New York: Miramax, 2002, p. 57.
48. Quoted in Miramax Books, *Gangs of New York*, p. 122.
49. Quoted in Miramax Books, *Gangs of New York*, p. 121.
50. Roger Ebert, "Catch Me If You Can," *Chicago Sun-Times*, December 25, 2002. http://rogerebert.suntimes.com/apps/pbcs.dll/article?AID=/20021225/REVIEWS/212250301/1023.
51. Quoted in Joal Ryan, "Leo 'Vindicated' in Lawsuit," E! Online, September 29, 2004. www.eonline.com/uberblog/b48356_leo_vindicated_in_lawsuit.html#ixzz0wt453reS.
52. Quoted in Ryan, "Leo 'Vindicated' in Lawsuit."
53. Quoted in AskMen.com, "Leonardo DiCaprio's Slash Horror," June 30, 2005. www.askmen.com/celebs/entertainment-news/leonardo-dicaprio/leonardo-dicaprio-slash-horror.html.

Chapter 5: Off-Camera Causes

54. Leonardo DiCaprio, "Bio," Twitter.com. https://twitter.com/ LeoDiCaprio.

55. Roger Friedman, "Leonardo DiCaprio's Eco Movie Bombs," Fox News, September 5, 2007. www.foxnews.com/ story/0,2933,295768,00.html.

56. Quoted in Jeanne Wolf, "Leonardo DiCaprio: Fame Can Make You 'a Little Bit Nuts,'" *Parade*, February 16, 2010. www. parade.com/celebrity/celebrity-parade/2010/0216-leonardo-dicaprio-shutter-island.html.

57. Quoted in *Nightline*, "Leading Man Leads a 'Green Revolution,'" ABC News, August 10, 2007. http://abcnews. go.com/Nightline/story?id=3466584&page=2.

58. Quoted in Ruben E. Nepales, "The Truth About Leo and His Reported RP Visit," *Philippine Daily Inquirer*, July 22, 2010. http:// showbizandstyle.inquirer.net/entertainment/entertainment/ view/20100722-282564/The-truth-about-Leo-and-his-reported-RP-visit.

59. Friedman, "Leonardo DiCaprio's Eco Movie Bombs."

60. Leonardo DiCaprio, *Water Planet*. www.leonardodicaprio.org.

61. Leonardo DiCaprio, *Global Warming*. www.leonardo dicaprio.org.

62. Quoted in WWF China, "WWF Announces Partnership with Leonardo DiCaprio to Save Tigers Now," May 27, 2010. www. wwfchina.org/english/loca.php?loca=677.

63. Leonardo DiCaprio, Afterword, in Richard Sobol, *Breakfast in the Rainforest: A Visit with Mountain Gorillas*. Cambridge, MA: Candlewick, 2008, p. 44.

64. Quoted in Leonardo DiCaprio.org, "Leonardo Donates $1 Million to the Clinton Bush Haiti Fund," press release. www.leonardo dicaprio.org/files/images/home/haiti_donation_block.png.

65. Quoted in Rader, "Leonardo DiCaprio, Hollywood Outsider."

Chapter 6: Leo Today, Leo Tomorrow

66. Quoted in Screenplay, Inc., "IMAX: Hubble 3D," IMDB.com. www.imdb.com/video/screenplay/vi2316175129.

67. Quoted in Roger Ebert, "Leonardo DiCaprio: 'I Like Characters Who Aren't Always What They Seem,'" *Chicago Sun-Times*, February 5, 2010. http://rogerebert.suntimes.com/apps/pbcs.dll/article?AID=/20100215/PEOPLE/100219984.

68. A.O. Scott, "All at Sea, Surrounded by Red Herrings," *New York Times*, February 19, 2010. http://movies.nytimes.com/2010/02/19/movies/19shutter.html?ref=movies.

69. Claudia Puig, "You Definitely Won't Sleep Through Complex Thriller 'Inception,'" *USA Today*, July 16, 2010. www.usatoday.com/life/movies/reviews/2010-07-15-inception15_ST_N.htm.

70. Quoted in John Hiscock, "Leonardo DiCaprio Interview," *Telegraph* (London), February 12, 2010. www.telegraph.co.uk/culture/film/7220114/Leonardo-DiCaprio-interview.html.

71. Quoted in Hiatt, "Leo Faces His Demons," p. 50.

72. Quoted in Cal Fussman, "10 Essential Lessons from Leo DiCaprio," *Esquire*, February 11, 2010. www.esquire.com/the-side/qa/dicaprio-interview-0310#ixzz0v6Kea5sM".

73. Quoted in Hiatt, "Leo Faces His Demons," p. 86.

74. Quoted in Hiatt, "Leo Faces His Demons," p. 86.

75. Quoted in Wolf, "Leonardo DiCaprio."

76. Quoted Smith and Ansen, "Hollywood Royalty."

77. Quoted in Scott, *Leonardo DiCaprio*, p. 2.

78. Quoted in Hiatt, "Leo Faces His Demons," p. 48.

79. Quoted in Thompson, *Leonardo DiCaprio*, p. 41.

1974

Leonardo Wilhelm DiCaprio is born November 11, 1974, in Los Angeles, California; his parents, George and Irmelin DiCaprio, separate less than a year later.

1988

Lands his first commercial, for Matchbox cars.

1991

Joins the cast of the hit sitcom *Growing Pains*, playing a homeless boy named Luke Bower.

1993

Makes breakthrough appearance opposite Robert De Niro in *This Boy's Life*; appears opposite Johnny Depp in *What's Eating Gilbert Grape?* and is nominated for both an Academy Award and a Golden Globe for this role.

1996

Appears in *Romeo + Juliet* and *Marvin's Room*.

1997

Appears in *Titanic*, the most expensive movie ever made; *Empire* magazine lists him as one of the "Top 100 Movie Stars of All Time"; chosen by *People* magazine as one of the "50 Most Beautiful People in the World."

2000

After a two-year hiatus from acting, appears in *The Beach*.

2002

After another two-year absence from the screen, appears in *Gangs of New York* and *Catch Me If You Can*.

2003

Receives an Environmental Leadership Award from Global Green.

2004

Plays Howard Hughes in *The Aviator*, a role that earns him the Golden Globe for Best Actor and his second Academy Award nomination; joins the board of directors of the Natural Resources Defense Council and Global Green USA.

2006

Appears in *The Departed* and *Blood Diamond*; nominated for a Golden Globe for both films and for an Academy Award for *Blood Diamond*.

2007

Narrates the documentary *The 11th Hour*; named by *Empire* magazine one of the "100 Sexiest Movie Stars" and by *Time* magazine one of the "100 Most Influential People in the World".

2008

Appears in *Body of Lies* and *Revolutionary Road*, along with his co-star from *Titanic* and longtime friend Kate Winslet.

2010

Appears in *Shutter Island* and *Inception*.

For More Information

Books

Nancy Krulik, *Leonardo DiCaprio: A Biography*. New York: Pocket, 1998. This early account covers DiCaprio's life and career through his rise to worldwide fame after the success of *Titanic*.

Miramax Books, *Gangs of New York: Making the Movie*. New York: Miramax, 2002. This companion to the film contains numerous full-page photographs, interviews with the director and the stars, and the complete screenplay.

Martin Noble, *Leonardo DiCaprio: An Unofficial Biography*. Woodbridge, England: Funfax, 1998. This book chronicles DiCaprio's early career, from his television appearances through his role in the blockbuster *Titanic*.

Brian J. Robb, *The Leonardo DiCaprio Album*. London: Plexus, 1998. This biography examines the life and early work of Leonardo DiCaprio.

Richard Sobol, *Breakfast in the Rainforest: A Visit with Mountain Gorillas*. Cambridge, MA: Candlewick, 2008. Leonardo DiCaprio wrote the afterword for this book detailing the plight of the critically endangered mountain gorillas. Contains numerous striking color photographs.

Douglas Thompson, *Leonardo DiCaprio*. New York: Berkeley Boulevard Books, 1998. A well-written and comprehensive biography of DiCaprio, with over sixty color photographs.

Periodicals

Leonardo DiCaprio, "Get Wise to Global Warming," *Time*, April 26, 2000.

Roger Ebert, "Leonardo DiCaprio: 'I Like Characters Who Aren't Always What They Seem,'" *Chicago Sun-Times*, February 5, 2010.

Brian Hiatt, "Leo Faces His Demons," *Rolling Stone*, August 5, 2010.

John Hiscock, "Leonardo DiCaprio Interview," *Telegraph* (London), February 12, 2010.

James Mottram, "Leonardo DiCaprio on Saving the World, Both on and off the Screen," *Herald* (Scotland), July 5, 2010.

Ruben E. Nepales, "The Truth About Leo and His Reported RP Visit," *Philippine Daily Inquirer*, July 22, 2010.

Anne-Marie O'Neill, "Riding the Wave," *People*, January 26, 1998.

Joel Stein, "Cinema: What's Eating Leonardo DiCaprio?" *Time*, February 21, 2000.

Jeanne Wolf, "Leonardo DiCaprio: Fame Can Make You 'a Little Bit Nuts,'" *Parade*, February 16, 2010.

Internet Sources

People, "Leonardo DiCaprio." www.people.com/people/leonardo_dicaprio.

Dotson Rader, "Leonardo DiCaprio, Hollywood Outsider," *Sunday Times* (London), January 11, 2009. http://entertainment.timesonline.co.uk/tol/arts_and_entertainment/film/article5467287.ece.

Sean Smith and David Ansen, "Hollywood Royalty," *Newsweek*, January 29, 2007. www.msnbc.msn.com/id/16720751/site/newsweek.

Websites

Leonardo DiCaprio (www.leonardodicaprio.com). The official Leonardo DiCaprio website has information on his latest films and provides links to his Twitter and Facebook pages, as well as to the Save Tigers Now campaign.

LeonardoDiCaprio.org (www.leonardodicaprio.org). Provides a wealth of information about the environment, renewable energy, and endangered species, as well as links to environmental campaigns and other environmental websites.

About the Author

Cherese Cartlidge holds a bachelor's degree in psychology and a master's degree in education. She currently works as a writer and editor and has written numerous books for children and young adults. In her spare time, she enjoys watching movies, and *Titanic* and *Catch Me If You Can* rank as two of her all-time favorites. She lives in Georgia with her two children, Thomas and Olivia.